TEACHING GENRE

Exploring 9 Types of Literature to Develop Lifelong Readers and Writers

by Tara McCarthy

S C H O L A S T I C
PROFESSIONAL BOOKS

New York • Toronto • London • Auckland • Sydney

ACKNOWLEDGMENTS

Poem #242 "I'll tell you how the sun rose" by Emily Dickinson from THE POEMS OF EMILY DICKINSON, Thomas H. Johnson, ed., Cambridge, Mass., The Belknap Press of Harvard University Press. Copyright ©1951, 1955, 1979, 1983 by the President and Fellows of Harvard College. Reprinted by permission of the publishers and Trustees of Amherst College.

"The Bat-Poet" from THE BAT-POET by Randall Jarrell. Copyright ©1963, 1965 by Randall Jarrell. Published by Michael di Capua Books/HarperCollins Publishers. Permission granted by Rhoda Weyr Agency, NY.

Excerpt from KIDS AT WORK: Lewis Hine and the Crusade Against Child Labor. Text copyright ©1994 Russell Freedman. Reprinted by permission of Clarion Books/Houghton Mifflin Co. All rights reserved.

From CELIA'S ISLAND JOURNAL by Loretta Krupinski. Copyright ©1992 by Loretta Krupinski. By permission of Little, Brown and Company.

"Pepper and Succotash" from A CELEBRATION OF FAMILY FOLKLORE by Steven J. Zeitlin, Amy J. Kotkin, and Holly Cutting Baker. Copyright ©1982 by Smithsonian Institution. Reprinted by permission of Pantheon Books, a division of Random House, Inc.

Excerpts from POWWOW by George Ancona. Copyright ©1953 by George Ancona. Reprinted by permission of Harcourt Brace & Company.

Excerpt from ADAM OF THE ROAD by Elizabeth Janet Gray. Illustrated by Robert Lawson. Copyright ©1942 by Elizabeth Janet Gray and Robert Lawson, renewed ©1970 by Elizabeth Janet Gray and John Boyd, Executor of the Estate of Robert Lawson. Used by permission of Viking Penguin, a division of Penguin Books USA Inc.

Excerpt from THE DARK-THIRTY by Patricia C. McKissack. Text copyright ©1992 by Patricia C. McKissack. Reprinted by permission of Random House, Inc.

Excerpt from A RIDE ON THE RED MARE'S BACK by Ursula K. Le Guin, illustrated by Julie Downing. Text copyright ©1992 by Ursula K. Le Guin. Illustrations copyright ©1992 Julie Downing. Reprinted by permission of the publisher, Orchard Books, New York.

Cover design by Vincent Ceci and Jaime Lucero
Cover illustration by Jo Lynn Alcorn
Interior design by Sydney Wright
Interior illustration by Jo Lynn Alcorn and Sydney Wright

ISBN 0-590-60345-0

Contents

To the Teacher

An increasing number of teachers in the middle grades are using literary genres as a framework for instruction in reading and writing. The genre approach appeals to middle-grade students because it is different from and more sophisticated than the approaches used in primary grades. As students work with genres, they call upon and develop their metacognitive abilities. They look not only at the "what"—the written products—but also at the "why's" and "how's," that is, at a writer's goals and strategies. In doing so, students become more insightful as readers, more concise as critics, and more successful as writers.

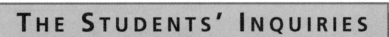

THE STUDENTS' INQUIRIES

In the middle grades, students are developing specific tastes and preferences concerning literature, and may ask demanding questions. Before reading, a student may ask not only, "What's this piece of literature about?" but also, "Is it fiction or nonfiction?" "How does it reflect my interests?" "Will I learn something that's important to me?" After reading, the student may ask, "Why did I like (or not like) this piece of literature?" "What was the author trying to do?" "Did she or he succeed?" "Do I want to try writing a piece like this? If so, what are some guidelines for writers to follow?" The questions above are related to genre, and move recursively through four areas of inquiry, as shown below:

1

The reader's personal response to a piece of literature.

2

The reader's understanding of the formal elements of the genre of the literature.

3

The reader's newly informed critique of the literature as an example of its genre.

4

The reader's ability to assess or create other examples of the genre.

Through whole-language approaches in earlier grades, most students have had a lot of experience with 1 and 4. Through concentrating now on genres, that is, on 2 and 3, students add a vital dimension to their enjoyment of literature and to their own skills in writing.

How This Book is Organized

The nine units deal with distinct genres or subgenres of literature: **Poetry**, Nonfiction including **Biography, Autobiography, Reports of Information,** Fiction including **Realistic Fiction in a Modern Setting, Historical Fiction, Folk Literature, Mystery, Modern Fantasy and Science Fiction.**

You can take the units up in the sequence above, organize your own sequence, or take up units as they seem to fit in with special curricular needs. For example:

✴ Use Reports of Information and Biography in conjunction with students' science reading, research, and writing.

✴ Use Realistic Fiction in a Modern Setting and/or Folk Literature in conjunction with social studies projects that call for multicultural perspectives.

✴ Use Historical Fiction and Autobiography in conjunction with projects about real-life heroes and heroines and the times they lived in.

Unit Organization

✴ Each unit begins with an **Overview** for the teacher that summarizes the essential characteristics of the genre.

✴ Next come **Pre-Reading Activities** that help students recall and organize their previous reading in the genre, and share their ideas about how the examples are alike.

✴ In **Reading and Responding**, students read an excerpt from literature in the genre and note their responses to it, using a reproducible response guide.

✴ The **Responding Options** section suggest several strategies that help students share their responses, dig deeper into the literary excerpt, and then identify and state major characteristics of the genre it represents.

✳ **Synthesizing and Applying** suggests on-going, multi-modal activities that will enrich students' enjoyment of the genre. At least one of the activities involves writing.

Highlights

✳ **Reproducibles:** Literature, Response Guides, Graphic Organizers

✳ **A Range of Activities** from easy to challenging

✳ **Provision for Activities** involving whole class, large and small groups, partners, individuals

✳ **An Annotated Bibliography (pages 102–111)** of recommended books, organized by genre, with content overviews and suggestions for the classroom

There is a special built-in "highlight" for you, as a teacher: As your students explore literature through genres and thus grow in their ability to think and talk incisively about literature, you are likely to find their discussions instructive for you, too. You will often feel like a learner as well as a leader, a participant as well as a mentor. You'll have numerous opportunities to share your own love of literature and to tell about great books you've read and why you like them.

CHAPTER 1

Poetry

TEACHER OVERVIEW

The web below shows the major characteristics of poetry in general, and a formal difference between narrative poetry and lyric poetry. Because there are so many lap-overs between the two kinds, this unit emphasizes the general characteristics of poetry.

Uses word pictures to build sensory impressions and create images

Plays with the sounds of words and the rhythms of phrases

POETRY

Usually **compresses** ideas: poetry uses less "space" than prose does to tell about an idea

Is usually intended to be read aloud

Lyric Poetry is meant to reveal the poet's feelings and unique reactions.

Narrative Poetry is meant to tell a story.

PRE-READING ACTIVITIES

1. Poetry Sleuthing

This activity can challenge students to inquire about poetry in a new way, and at the same time provide you with an overview of what students already know about the genre.

✳ Without using the words <u>poem</u> or <u>poetry</u>, write on the chalkboard and read aloud to the class two very different examples of the genre. Examples are given below. (The limerick is "Anonymous," and the second is from a poem by Emily Dickinson.) Ask students to listen and to read along silently.

> **A.** *A diner, once dining at Crewe,*
> *Found quite a large mouse in his stew.*
> *Said the waiter, "Don't shout*
> *And wave it about,*
> *Or the rest will be wanting one too!"*

> **B.** *I'll tell you how the sun rose,—*
> *A ribbon at a time.*
> *The steeples swam in amethyst,*
> *The news like squirrels ran.*
>
> *The hills untied their bonnets,*
> *The bobolinks* begun.*
> *Then I said softly to myself,*
> *'That must have been the sun!'*

✳ Ask students to discuss how these pieces of literature are alike. Most students will agree first that they are both poems. Encourage the class to tell how they know. Students may suggest characteristics such as short lines, rhyme, and rhythm. Note students' ideas on poster paper or on the chalkboard.

✳ Students can move on to a discussion of how the two poems are different. Help students notice

Different Tones. The first poem is "funny"; the second is "serious."

* An American migratory song bird

Different Rhythms. To illustrate, read the poems aloud with students and place accent marks over the accented syllables.

Different Rhythm Patterns. Ask students to identify the end-rhymes in the first poem. Underline them (Crewe, stew, too; shout, about). Advise students that the rhymes in the Dickinson poem are "tricky." Point out <u>begun</u> and <u>sun</u> in the second and last lines of the second stanza, then have students say the end words—<u>time</u> and <u>ran</u>—in the second and last lines of the first stanza. *Ask:* Did the poet feel that she had to use **exact** rhymes in this poem?

Different Ways of Approaching a Subject. Ask students: Which poem is more like a story? (the limerick) Which poem is more like a painting of a wondrous, everyday event? (the Dickinson poem)

Different Purposes. *Ask:* Which poem do you think is meant to reveal the poet's personal views and feelings? (the Dickinson poem) Why do you think so? What do you think is the purpose of the other poem? (to have fun with rhymes; to amuse people)

Conclude the activity by asking students to write the following question in their journals: <u>What is a poem?</u> Encourage students to work independently or with a partner to jot down some ideas they have about the answer. Explain that they can add and change ideas as they read and discuss other poems, and that there are many possible answers to the question. Now and then, check students' progress with these notes; they will need to refer to them in carrying out one of the *Synthesizing and Applying* activities.

2. Drawing on Previous Experiences with Poetry

Invite students to tell about poems they've enjoyed. Prompt them with questions such as: What is the first poem you remember hearing as a child? Did you like the poem? Explain why or why not. What are some poems or rhymes that you say aloud when you're playing games? Name a poem that makes you laugh, think or wonder, look at something in a new way. Who is your favorite poet? Why? Have you written your own poems? Tell about one that you especially enjoyed writing. Conclude the activity by asking students what subjects poets deal with. List students' ideas on the chalkboard. Some examples are people, animals, nature, funny incidents, stories about heroes and heroines, problems, feelings, and a new way of looking at something.

To help students discover what makes a poem on these subjects different from prose, *ask:* Can writers tell about all these things in prose, too, that is, in stories, novels and reports?

READING AND RESPONDING

✸ Distribute copies of the poem on page 12, which appears in the book *The Bat-Poet* by Randall Jarrell. Explain that the book tells about a young bat who writes poems about various animals in the woods and fields, and finally—just before it's time for him to hibernate for the winter—a poem about himself. (*The Bat-Poet* is a good read-aloud book, full of humor, insights into the natural world, and hints about strategies for writing poetry.)

✸ Read the poem aloud to students as they follow along silently.

✸ Distribute **The Bat-Poet Response Guide**. Review the questions and prompts with the class. Ask students to work with a partner to read the poem aloud once more. Explain that students can then write their responses independently or with their partners.

The Bat-Poet

by Randall Jarrell

A bat is born
Naked and blind and pale.
His mother makes a pocket of her tail
And catches him. He clings to her long fur
By his thumbs and toes and teeth.
And then the mother dances through the night
Doubling and looping, soaring, somersaulting—
Her baby hangs on underneath.
All night, in happiness, she hunts and flies.
Her high sharp cries
Like shining needlepoints of sound
Go out into the night and, echoing back,
Tell her what they have touched.
She hears how far it is, how big it is,
Which way it's going:
She lives by hearing.
The mother eats the moths and gnats she catches
In full flight; in full flight
The mother drinks the water of the pond
She skims across. Her baby hangs on tight.
Her baby drinks the milk she makes him
In moonlight or starlight, in mid-air.
Their single shadow, printed on the moon
Or fluttering across the stars,
Whirls on all night; at daybreak
The tired mother flaps home to her rafter.
The others all are there.
They hang themselves up by their toes,
They wrap themselves in their brown wings.
Bunched upside down, they sleep in air.
Their sharp ears, their sharp teeth, their
        quick sharp faces
Are dull and slow and mild.
All the bright day, as the mother sleeps,
She folds her wings about her sleeping child.

The Bat-Poet
RESPONSE GUIDE

Name: _____

1. What feelings do you have as you read and listen to the poem? _____

_____

_____

2. In your own words, tell what is going on in the poem. _____

_____

_____

3. On the lines below, copy the part of the poem you liked best and tell why.

_____

_____

_____

_____

_____

_____

_____

_____

_____

_____

4. While this poem is about a bat, does it remind you of something else you know about?
Explain. _____

_____

_____

_____

Responding Options

When students revisit a poem with your guidance, they can develop an awareness of the craft of poetry, that is, of <u>how</u> the poem makes them react as they do. At the same time, by keeping your questions open-ended, you allow students to focus on their enjoyment and appreciation of the poem. Use *The Bat-Poet* **Response Guide** questions to aid revisiting.

1. *Encourage Students to Share Their Responses* Invite students to share their responses to the first question. Accept all responses, but help students to develop them with specifics. For example:

> <u>Student</u>: When I read the poem, I feel happy.
>
> <u>Teacher</u>: Why is that? Please read us some lines that make you feel especially happy.

2. *Interpret the Action* In response to the second question, most students may be quite literal: A mother bat takes her baby with her as she hunts for insects each night; then the mother, with her baby, goes home to sleep during the day. Help students identify lines and phrases that make these simple actions vivid. For example you might say:

In the sixth line, the poet says the mother "dances" through the night. What words in the next line remind you of dancing? Let's look through the poem again to find other words that paint pictures of movement (<u>in full flight</u>, <u>skims</u>, <u>fluttering</u>, <u>whirls</u>, <u>flaps</u>). Have students find word pictures in the last part of the poem that tell about slow, sleepy actions, as compared with swift, dancing flight. (Examples begin with "The tired mother flaps home to her rafter.")

Ask students: "What do you think of the line 'Like shining needlepoints of sound'? What is the poet describing here?" (the bat's 'sharp cries,' or echolocation system)

3. *Identify Elements of Poetry* Invite students to read aloud the lines they've copied in response to the third question on the **Response Guide**, and to tell why they like these lines. Then reread aloud the lines that students have selected and help them discover the qualities that make the lines poetic. The major qualities are suggested below. You'll want to adjust your discussion prompts to your students' level of understanding.

Words with similar sounds:
- ✳ Alliteration: "By his <u>th</u>umbs and <u>t</u>oes and <u>t</u>eeth."
- ✳ "<u>S</u>ingle <u>Sh</u>adow:" "<u>T</u>ell her what she has <u>t</u>ouched."
- ✳ Assonance: "They <u>wra</u>p themselves in their bro<u>wn</u> <u>wings</u>."

Repetition:
- ✳ ". . . how far it is, how big it is,"
- ✳ "In full flight; in full flight"

* "They hang themselves up . . . ./They wrap themselves. . . ./
  . . . they sleep in air."

Rhyme: Jarrell uses rhyme where it fits, but doesn't insist upon it. Examples of end-rhymes occurring at different intervals:

* lines 2 and 3 (pale/tail)
* lines 5 and 8 (teeth/underneath)
* lines 9 and 10 (flies/cries).

Ask students to look through the poem to find other end-rhymes, such as flight/tight, mid-air/ there, mild/child.

Imagery: Reread some lines to demonstrate how the poet is seeing his subject like "takes" in a movie. Sometimes he sees the bat in a "long action," and makes a long line with long words to capture the picture: "Doubling and looping, soaring, somersaulting—."

Sometimes the poet sees short, abrupt actions, and makes shorter lines with shorter words:

"She hears how far it is, how big it is,

Which way it's going:

She lives by hearing."

4. Connect the Poem with Previous Experiences Responses to the fourth question on the **Response Guide** may vary widely. Many students may simply say that the poem reminds them of other nighttime animals, or of other animals and their young, or of their own bat sightings. Some students, however, may pick up on themes of motherly love, of a trusting infant, of the regular patterns of nature, or of how natural beings that we've been led to believe are dangerous and scary can actually be harmless and beautiful. You might diverge from this particular poem at this point to ask students about other poems they've read that helped them see things in a new way.

5. Summarize General Ideas About Poetry Invite students to summarize general ideas about poetry that they've discussed as they worked with this poem. Write ideas on the chalkboard and encourage students to copy them under the "What is a poem?" heading in their journals. Examples:

* Many poems tell about ordinary events.
* A poem may stir up deep feelings in the readers.
* Poems use the sounds of language in deliberate, special ways.

6. Hold Choral Readings Invite interested students to form choral reading groups and arrange the poem from *The Bat-Poet* to read aloud to the class. Remind groups to attend to punctuation, thought groups, and rhyming lines as they determine how to divide the poem into sections:

Which parts will be solos, which read by duos, and which read by a larger group? You may wish to have the class agree on criteria by which they will assess the choral readings.

SYNTHESIZING AND APPLYING

1. **Compare Poetry and Prose** Suggest that students find and study a factual prose or visual/oral account of bats and compare it with the Jarrell poem. Students can find factual material in nature encyclopedias, CD-ROM science units, nonfiction trade books, and natural history videotapes.

Ask students to focus their research on two aspects of bat behavior: how bats bear and care for their young; and how bats get their food. Students might summarize their findings and insights in a chart. *Example:*

Bats in Poetry and Prose

	Poetry from *The Bat-Poet*	Prose from *World Book* article "Bats"
Gives facts about bats	some facts about a particular bat	lots of facts about many kinds of bats
Uses word pictures	a great many	some
Shows the writer's feelings about bats	definitely; the writer likes bats	no; can't tell; objective report
Uses the sounds of language to get the reader's attention	definitely	no
Reminds me of aspects of human life	yes	not really
Is enjoyed most when read aloud	yes	no
Would be useful in writing a science report about bats	maybe	yes
Tells me things about bats that I didn't know before	some	yes
Helps me think about bats in a new way	yes	yes

As students share their charts, encourage them to support some of their entries with examples from poetry and prose. As a result of class discussion, students should be able to add notes to "What is a poem?" in their journals.

2. *Encourage Students to Relate Poetry to Everyday Life and to Classroom Experiences*
There's hardly a subject or skill you'll take up in the classroom that does not have a poem relating to it somewhere in the literature. If you make poetry anthologies a permanent part of your classroom resource bank, students can refer to the anthologies to find poems relating to geography, science, history, health and athletics, cross-cultural understanding, mathematics, values, friendship, and community concerns. Ask students to find and share poems that relate to these areas as the class studies them. Sharing can be done through reading the poems aloud or by copying them for inclusion in relevant displays, reports, and booklets. Always ask students how the poems add to their understanding of, and feelings about, the subjects they've been studying.

3. *Have a Poetry Read-Aloud Every Day* Begin and/or end each day with a poem for students to listen to. Vary the poems—a humorous poem by Shel Silverstein, a lyric by Dickinson or Rossetti, a rousing narrative poem such as "The Highwayman," or a moody, insightful poem by Robert Frost. Have students help you choose poems and take turns reading them to the class. Make time for reactions from the audience: What did they like about the poem? What did it remind them of?

4. *Encourage Students to Write Poems Frequently* As a warm-up, have the class create a poem together to answer their journal question, "What is a poem?" Each student can offer a line based on his or her notes while you write the class poem on the chalkboard. *Example:*

What Is a Poem?

Maybe it rhymes and maybe it doesn't.
Words fit together with sounds that sing.
I feel something new when I read a poem.
A feeling like happy, sad, or surprised.
Poems tell such stories:
A bat flies, the sun sets, a man finds a mouse in his stew.
It could happen to me or you.
In a poem, it is always new.
A poem makes you see things freshly, as if you just woke up.

After this warm-up, point out to students that they can write poems independently about any experience they have or observation they make. Suggest some off-beat subjects for students to approach through poetry, such as colors on a map, a school lunch, a fish in the classroom aquarium, different kinds of sneakers, a glitch in the school PA system, a substitute teacher, a missing mitten or glove, a water fountain, a new student, a school bus with a flat tire, a stray dog, or an empty shopping cart on the sidewalk.

5. *Help Students Find Ways to Share Their Own Poems* As your students become comfortable with poetry and begin to think of it as a natural way of expressing feelings and sharing ideas and images, encourage them to enter the poems they like best in a class anthology. A-poem-a-week is a reasonable request to make of each student. Students may wish to work with partners occasionally to refine their poems, or may want to get feed-back from a small group before submitting the poem. Ask students to look through the anthology each week, find a classmate's poem that they especially like, tell why they like it, and then read the poem aloud to the class.

Students can make copies of their anthology for the library, read selected poems to students in other classrooms, hold a Poetry Day for family and friends, or make a video- or audiotape of poetry readings.

6. *Encourage Students to Memorize Poems They Like* Your students are still at the age when memorization is easy, and for many people there's nothing as great as being able to recite all or part of a beloved poem that they learned "by heart" when they were young.

Ask students to find a poem that they want to keep in their minds forever. Once they have written the poem in their journals, they may want to give a copy of it to a classmate-coach to help them practice. Then have them recite the poem to a larger group. Suggested follow-ups to use with the class audience might include:

✳ Discuss what makes the poem a poem.

✳ Discuss what's fun and what's difficult about memorizing a poem.

✳ Discuss what ideas and images in the poem make it worth memorizing by heart.

CHAPTER 2

Nonfiction
Biography

TEACHER OVERVIEW

As a genre, biography has the following characteristics:

1
Tells about a real person

2
Shows that the writer knows a lot about this person

BIOGRAPHY

3
Describes the person's environment

4
Provides anecdotes or details that show the person in action

5
Shows how the person affects other people

6
States or implies how the writer feels about the person

PRE-READING ACTIVITIES

1. Brainstorming First-Hand Biography

Because almost all of us know a few people whose lives we have witnessed fairly intimately, the characteristics of biography are usually easy for students to comprehend, especially if they begin to explore the genre through first-hand biography.

A first-hand biography reveals another person through the eyes of a writer who has had an on-going, face-to-face relationship with the person. So, you might introduce the biography unit by (a) distributing copies of the biography web or replicating it on the chalkboard; (b) applying each characteristic of biography to someone you know personally. Example: (the numbers represent the characteristic each statement addresses.)

[1] Here's a brief **biography**, or **life story** of a real person, my Aunt Cindy. [2] She was a big part of my childhood. My parents and I visited her at least once a month. [3] I remember many visits to Aunt Cindy's tiny, dark apartment. It was very quiet in that building— maybe because tenants were not allowed to have children or pets. [4] In spite of that, Aunt Cindy found a way to express her love for animals: she spent her days working at an animal shelter near her home, and scouting out alleyways for stray cats and puppies and then finding homes for them. [5] Aunt Cindy was so earnest and enthusiastic about saving animals that she got all her family and most of her friends involved in her project. Together, we found good homes for at least 500 animals. [6] Aunt Cindy was old and frail, but she showed us that through love and determination one can accomplish a great deal.

After presenting your biography, invite volunteers to follow your model and the web to tell the class about someone significant in their own lives. Then engage students in a discussion around the following questions:

1. What makes the lives of certain people interesting to you?

2. What can you learn about a person by studying his or her life?

3. What might you learn about yourself by exploring someone else's life?

2. Drawing on Previous Experiences with Biography

Remind the class that biographies appear not only in books, but also in newspaper and magazine articles, in social studies texts and reference books, in television and movies, in radio features about famous people, in talks by guest speakers on special occasions such as Martin Luther King, Jr. Day, and via Internet pages. Have students work in groups of five or six to identify two or three biographies they have read, watched, or heard.

Ask groups to discuss what most impresses them about the true-life stories they've chosen. Most groups will focus on the achievements and events in the life of the biographee; a few groups—using the web on page 19 and your model as references—may focus on the way the writer presented the biography. Groups can appoint a spokesperson to explain their choices to the class. Conclude pre-reading by asking the class to brainstorm answers to the following questions:

✳ Suppose you wanted to write a biography about someone you yourself have never met. Whom would you choose? Why?

✳ What particular aspect of their life or achievement would you emphasize?

Note class responses on poster paper or the chalkboard for students to refer to later on.

READING AND RESPONDING

1. Distribute copies of the excerpt from Russell Freedman's *Kids at Work*. (If possible, make the book available for students to use throughout their study of biography.) Preface students' reading of the excerpt by explaining that Freedman's book is a biography of Lewis Hine, an American photographer who worked in the first half of the twentieth century. Hine was an investigative reporter as well as a photographer, and became a master of pictures that told stories in themselves. His main concern was for the young children who—because of their poverty—were forced to labor long hours in factories and mines. The children suffered from exhaustion, hunger, emotional neglect, and lack of schooling.

2. Distribute the *Kids at Work* **Response Guide**. Ask students to form groups of four or five. Group members will preview the guide, read the excerpt together, and discuss and decide upon responses. Encourage groups to note any varying responses to the questions.

Kids at Work
by Russell Freedman

Carrying a simple box camera like the one he used at Ellis Island, Lewis Hine traveled back and forth across the country, from the sardine canneries of Maine to the cotton fields of Texas. He took pictures of kids at work, listened to their stories, and reported on their lives.

His goal was to open the public's eyes to the horrors of child labor. He wanted to move people to action.

Hine wasn't concerned with children who worked at odd jobs after school or did chores around the house or the family farm. He didn't object to youngsters working as trainees and apprentices, learning skills they would use for the rest of their lives. The campaign against child labor was not directed against them. It was aimed at the exploitation of boys and girls as cheap labor.

"There is work that profits children, and there is work that brings profit only to employers," Hine said. "The object of employing children is not to train them, but to get high profits from their work."

Because children could be hired cheaply and were too small to complain, they were often employed to replace adult workers. In industries where large numbers of children were employed, their low wages pulled down the earnings of everyone else, so that grown-ups could not earn enough to support their families. As a result, poor families needed their children's wages just to survive.

Some people argued that child employees weren't really expected to work very hard. "Let me tell you right here," declared Hine, "that these [jobs] involve work, hard work, deadening in its monotony, exhausting physically . . . the worker's only joy [is getting paid]. We might even say of these children that they are condemned to work."

As criticism of child labor grew, a number of states passed laws regulating working hours and wages for children. But more often than not, those laws were filled with loopholes and favored the manufacturers. Some states failed to enforce even the weakest child-labor laws.

The National Child Labor Committee was fighting for strict laws and effective enforcement. Founded in 1904, it was a militant organization made up of men and women who believed that a healthy, happy, normal childhood was the rightful heritage of all children.

The NCLC wanted to ban the employment of children under fourteen years of age in most occupations, and under sixteen in dangerous trades like mining. For all children, the NCLC demanded an eight-hour day, no night work, and mandatory work permits based on documentary proof of age. The NCLC also wanted compulsory school-attendance laws, but it did not expend much effort on that seemingly impossible dream. It was tough enough to get honest child-labor laws passed and obeyed.

As Hine traveled, he discovered that investigating child labor was like entering an armed camp. Owners and managers regarded the little man with the big box camera as a troublemaker. Often they refused to let Hine into their plants. Angry foremen and factory police threatened him. In many places, child workers were kept out of sight, hidden from public view.

To gain access to factories, mines, sweatshops, and mills, and to use his camera freely, Hine often had to disguise his real purpose. His students at the Ethical Culture School knew him as a talented actor and mimic. He would entertain them during nature walks by impersonating a wayward tramp or an itinerant peddler. Now he changed the roles he played, posing as a fire inspector, or an insurance salesman, or an industrial photographer who was after pictures of buildings and factory machinery.

In a textile mill, he would set up his camera to photograph a loom, then ask a child to stand next to the loom so that Hine could get a sense of scale, showing the size of the machinery. When the photograph was printed, it emphasized the fact that the worker who tended that loom was indeed a small child.

Whenever possible, Hine tried to photograph the workplace itself. If he couldn't do that, he waited at the factory gates with his fifty pounds of camera equipment, then photographed the young workers as they entered and left the plant. He reported from Augusta, Georgia: "Entrance to the mill was extremely difficult. The man in charge absolutely refused to let me through, even as a visitor. So I waited close outside the main gate, concealed in the darkness of the woods, and at 6:00 P.M. I counted about thirty-five boys who appeared to be from nine to fourteen years of age. I stopped them and took them around the corner for a flash-powder photo. Some of the smallest boys said they had been working at the mill for several years."

Kids at Work
RESPONSE GUIDE

Names: _____   _____

_____   _____   _____

1. Is this excerpt a good example of biography? _____ Why or why not?

_____

_____

_____

_____

2. What is the biographer's goal? _____

_____

_____

_____

_____

3. What was Hine's goal? _____

_____

_____

_____

_____

4. What feelings did we have as we read about kids working in factories? _____

_____

_____

_____

_____

5. What facts in the excerpt impressed us most? _____

_____

_____

_____

Responding Options

1. _Share Responses_ Have groups present their responses and compare and contrast them with those of other groups. Ask group members to back up their answers with examples from the text.

2. _Identify Biographical Characteristics in the Excerpt_ Encourage groups to use the _Biography Web_ on page 19 to point out which characteristics of biography show up in the excerpt.

> _Examples:_
>
> ✳ Freedman uses many quotations from Hine's own writing which shows that Freedman researched Hine's life thoroughly.
>
> ✳ The details about the kinds of mills and about the children who worked in them tells a lot about children's environment in those days.

3. _Illustrate the Images_ Ask students to identify a phrase, sentence, or paragraph in the excerpt that particularly impresses them and to draw or paint a picture to accompany it, using the text as a caption.

4. _Conduct Mock Interviews_ Suggest that partners conduct questions/answer presentations modeled on TV interviews. There are different possibilities: the interviewer talks to Hine about his work; the interviewer talks to Freedman about his biography of Hine; Freedman talks to Hine about Hine's work.

Remind students that who-what-where-why-when-how questions elicit more interesting answers than questions that can be answered with a simple "yes" or "no."

Example: <u>What makes you angry about little kids working in factories?</u> as opposed to <u>Do you get angry about little kids working in factories?</u> Have partners plan, rehearse, and then present their interviews to the class. Ask the audience to listen for and comment on (1) factual statements based on material from the biography; (2) the feelings and attitudes of the interviewer and the interviewee.

SYNTHESIZING AND APPLYING

Focus on Feelings Help students understand that biographers generally choose to write about someone whose goals, ideas, actions, and achievements fill the writer with strong feelings, such as sympathy, admiration, curiosity, or intellectual excitement. Reinforce this concept by inviting students to brainstorm endings for the following sentence. (*Stress that sentence completions should begin with strong verbs, rather than with are.*)

Examples of sentence endings:

> I'm interested in people who . . . .
> > . . . <u>develop</u> ways to save rain forests (endangered animals; oceans; etc.)
> > . . . <u>teach</u> others how to be the "best they can be"
> > . . . <u>dare</u> to undertake adventures
> > . . . <u>care for or treat</u> people who are sick
> > . . . <u>work</u> hard for their communities
> > . . . <u>help</u> other people overcome hard times and difficult circumstances

Write their endings on the chalkboard.

Help Students Write First-Hand Biographies Build on the above activity, and your previous discussion, reading, and pre-reading activities on biography, to help students draft a first-hand biographical incident.

Introduce the writing activity:
Ask students to look at the notes they've made about the kinds of people they're interested in. Then have them think of someone they know personally who is like one of those people.

> *Example:* Uncle Fred is someone I know who shares his knowledge with others.

Set up some drafting ideas:
1. Name the person and tell why he or she interests you.
Example: Uncle Fred is the relative that entertains and impresses me with his bird stories.

2. Use visual imagery to show how the person moves, dresses, and speaks.
Example: Uncle Fred wears tattered pants, old shirts, and shoes with holes in the soles. He looks a little disorganized, but he isn't disorganized when he talks about birds! He can tell you every detail about every bird he's ever spotted in the park.

3. Tell about the subject's surroundings.
Example: Uncle Fred lives in an apartment building with concrete all around. He always complains about how his neighbors make so much noise that they drown out the sounds of the birds.

4. Tell about a typical routine or event in the subject's life.
Example: Each morning, Uncle Fred sets out with his binoculars and his Bird Notebook. He heads for the park. Sometimes he eats breakfast beforehand, but usually he just carries some bread with him, to share with the birds.

5. Use dialogue or quotations to show some typical remarks of the subject. (Refer students to the quotations Freedman uses in his biography of Hine.)

Example: "What are you doing all this for?" I asked my Uncle Fred on an especially snowy, cold day. "Well" he said, "It's just that I like to help these birds survive in winter. When the snow drifts are two feet high, there is no way the birds can find food for themselves. We have to bring it to them."

6. Compare and/or contrast the person to other people.

Example: In the snow-covered park, we met Meg. Like my uncle, she was throwing crumbs to the birds. To me, it looked like Meg could use a few crumbs herself. I watched other people pass by, all wrapped up in their coats and in themselves. Unlike Uncle Fred and Meg, they ignored the birds.

7. Close with sentences that show how the incident taught you something about the person and about yourself.

Example: I said, "Don't you get mad when other people don't feed the birds?" Uncle Fred looked at me kindly. "Sonny," he said, "life's too short to get mad at those who don't share your love for particular people, places, and things. It's enough to know that one person cares, and it looks like that person is you, because here you *are!*"

As an aid for writing partners as they assess drafts of one another's first-hand biographies, list the seven points, above, as guides for reading, conferencing, and revising. While all the points should be included in the first-hand biography, they need not appear in the sequence presented in the examples.

Set Up Biography Reading Groups Groups of five or six students can focus on biographies that represent a special interest of the group, such as science, adventure, pioneer days, or childhood in different cultures. So that students of different abilities can work together in each group, be sure to suggest or provide biographies at different reading levels. See the *Annotated Bibliography*, pages 103–104, for suggested titles.

Each group can decide beforehand what special characteristics of biography they will look for as they read. After reading, each group member can tell the group how the biography reflects, or fails to reflect, the characteristics.

Groups might share their reading experience with the class by presenting Biography Book-Talks, or by creating a bulletin board display called The Best in Biography.

Encourage Students to Research Real Lives and Tell About Them This can be an individual, partner, or small-group activity, and the product can take different forms, according to the abilities and interests of each student. *Examples:*

* ✸ a written biography of several pages

* ✸ an illustrated biography that highlights major events in the person's life and uses captions to tell about the pictured events

* ✸ a skit or a one-act play that focuses on one of the person's major achievements

* ✸ an audio- or videotape simulating an interview with the person

* ✸ a monologue in which the student acts the part of the person and tells about his or her life, from the first-person point of view

Preface the activity by reviewing the general characteristics of biography. Discuss different sources for finding out about a person's life, such as encyclopedias, biographical dictionaries, nonfiction books, periodicals, Internet resources, library picture files, and videotapes. Encourage your students to use several sources when doing their research.

CHAPTER 3

Autobiography

TEACHER OVERVIEW

Because autobiography and biography share many characteristics, you may wish to teach these genres in tandem or one after the other. Autobiography has the following characteristics:

The main character is the writer.

Recounts key incidents in the writer's life

AUTOBIOGRAPHY

Describes major influences (people, events, places) on the writer

Describes interactions between the writer and significant people in his or her life

Reveals the writer's feelings, reactions, values, and goals

PRE-READING ACTIVITIES

1. Brainstorming Different Autobiographical Forms

After explaining the etymology of the word (auto: self; bio: life; graph: write), invite students to recall different times and different ways in which they have told about their own lives. Since the objective of this activity is for students to realize that they have often told pieces of their life story, throw the net wide! Encourage students to reach back into their memories and list not only written pieces, but also examples of visual and oral forms that tell something about themselves. Write students' ideas on the chalkboard. They may include the following:

Written pieces: journals, diaries, letters to friends, reports about school activities, first-person stories about incidents that they have been involved in; poems about things they've seen, felt, or experienced.

Visual and oral forms: pictures and paintings that depict events or people they are familiar with; photo albums or videotapes that record important moments in their lives; skits and plays based on their life stories; informal anecdotes about their lives, shared in conversations with friends and family; tangible mementos and souvenirs, such as awards, seashells, or favorite childhood toys.

Conclude the brainstorming by asking: <u>Suppose you wanted to write your autobiography in the form of a book. How would you use the things we've listed here to get started?</u> Possible responses: put the items in chronological order, from when I was little to now; choose the things that are most important to me, and then write about <u>why</u> they're important; choose several of the items, and then ask my family what they remember about a particular incident.

2. Previewing Autobiographical Literature

Have a few examples of autobiographies by people whose names your students are likely to recognize available. Examples can be short, as from anthologies or periodicals, or book-length. See the *Annotated Bibliography*, page 104, for suggested titles. As you show the examples, give a brief description of each one. For example: "This is the autobiography of Beverly Cleary. You probably remember that Cleary is the author of the *Beezus* and *Ramona* books." Then invite students to discuss what they hope to learn through reading the autobiography. Write students' ideas on the chalkboard or on poster paper for reference.

Students may first suggest data such as year and place of birth, names of family members, where the writer went to school, etc. Prompt them to move on to what else the writer might reveal about his or her life. *Examples:*

✱ What important events does Cleary remember from her childhood?

✱ What people stand out in her memory? How did they influence her?

✱ What were her favorite things to do when she was a kid?

✱ What sorts of things happened to her (happy, sad, scary)?

✱ When did she start writing? What were her first stories about?

Next, focus on the purposes readers might have for reading the autobiography, in addition to finding out more about Beverly Cleary's life. *Examples:*

✱ to find out how families lived many years ago

✱ to find out how writers get ideas for stories

✱ to find out how Cleary and I are different and alike

Finally, focus on the purposes that Cleary and others might have for writing an autobiography. There are essentially two purposes and two audiences:

✱ to share one's experiences, ideas, goals, and feelings with a *wide audience*

✱ to record and make permanent for *oneself* the most significant events and memories in one's life so far

READING AND RESPONDING

Distribute copies of the following autobiographical pieces. Explain that the journal entries were written more than a hundred years ago by Celia Thaxter, a young girl who lived with her family on White Island, off the coast of New Hampshire, where her father was the lighthouse keeper. In the second piece, "Pepper and Succotash," Brian Gay, a modern-day eleven-year-old, recalls funny stories his father told.

Distribute the **Autobiography Response Guide** and review the questions with the class. Then ask students to work with a partner to read the pieces and enter their ideas on the guide.

Celia's Island Journal

January 17, 1841

The winters seem as long as a whole year. Sometimes to amuse ourselves we take pennies (for we have nothing to spend them on) and make round holes in the thick frost on the panes of glass by breathing on the coins until they are warm. Peeping out, we watch the boats scudding by. Sometimes we can even see the round head of a seal moving among the kelp-covered rocks.

March 3, 1843

We survive many a dreary winter by keeping to our fireside and living with the plants, singing birds, books, and playthings that Mother and Father were wise enough to bring from the mainland. For in the stormy winter, no supply boats venture out to us. Father holds school at the kitchen table. He is teaching us reading and arithmetic. Most of all, I like to listen to Father recite poetry written by famous people.

September 20, 1845

My father often sails away to visit other islands, and sometimes he does not return home until dark. The lighthouse has no way to light the dark boathouse below, for its beams are sent far out to sea. So when the boat is out late, I light a lantern and go down to the water's edge. With the lantern at my feet, I sit waiting in the darkness, knowing my little light will guide Father home. I am always glad to hear the creaking of the mast and the rattling of the oarlocks as his boat draws near.

Pepper and Succotash

When I was little my father used to make up stories to tell me and my brother about two twin red-headed boys named Pepper and Succotash. This was purely an individual art form. He would never know when he started out how the story was going to end up. He would just spin these yarns.

One time he told us the story of Pepper and Succotash going to Mars. I don't remember how they got there but all the people would have some kind of bubble gum and they would chew it and blow bubbles out of their ears and go floating around. The bubbles were something like helium. There were witches and the boys would chew this bubble gum and float away from the witches.

Another time Pepper and Succotash went down to the river on a picnic. There was no way to get across so they took a whole string of hot dogs and they made it into a lasso and threw it across the river to a stump. And then they monkey-walked across, you know, they had to hang. When they got across they ate all of the hot dogs and then after they had finished the picnic they didn't know how to get back over the stream. So one of them pulled out the plug and they walked across.

Brian R. Gay, Age 11, Washington, DC.

Autobiography
RESPONSE GUIDE

Partners' names: _____ _____

Writer: **Celia Thaxter**

1. Do you think that Celia enjoyed living in a lighthouse? Support your idea with specific details from her journal. _____

_____

_____

_____

2. How would you describe Celia? _____

_____

_____

3. Why do you think Celia kept a journal during her "lighthouse years" (who do you think she was writing for)? _____

_____

_____

_____

Writer: **Brian R. Gray**

4. Why do you think the "Pepper and Succotash" stories are important to Brian?

_____

_____

5. If you met Brian, what questions or ideas would you like to explore with him?

_____

_____

_____

Responding Options

1. Share Responses Have partners discuss their responses with two or three other teams. Suggest that this larger group appoint a spokesperson to present the group's ideas to the class. Individual and partner responses will vary. For example, some students may feel that Celia's life was lonely or boring, while others may feel it was full of interesting activities. Welcome varying responses and encourage students to discuss and debate them.

2. Identify the Autobiographical Elements in the Excerpts During class discussion, note students' ideas about what Celia and Brian reveal about themselves and in what ways they think the authors are alike. Ideas will vary but responses might include

* people and events that the authors remember vividly;

* expressed or implied feelings about these people and events;

* their personal involvement with key events and people;

* what the authors, as writers, are like as people, for example <u>observant</u>, <u>humorous</u>, or <u>loving</u>.

Conclude this responding step by directing students' attention to your chalkboard notes. Ask students to discuss how the items on the list make Celia's and Brian's writing <u>autobiographical</u>. At this point, you may wish to distribute copies of the *Autobiography Web* on page 29. Students can use the web to substantiate their understandings about the autobiographical nature of the two examples.

3. Brainstorm Autobiographical Events Since "privacy" is a big issue in many communities, you may wish to stress that publishing autobiographical material is entirely optional: There is much writing we do just for ourselves and don't wish to share with anyone else. Explain that, in contrast, Celia Thaxter (who eventually became a poet) delighted in her childhood writing and was eager to have it made public; and that Brian Gay happily contributed his story-memories to a book about "family folklore." You might ask each student to make a short list of personal events he or she would like to share with a wide audience of readers. In this context, you can loop back to and revisit autobiographers' purposes and audiences (page 31).

SYNTHESIZING AND APPLYING

1. *Read and Critique Autobiographies* Critiquing according to guidelines not only provides a way for students to focus on the characteristics of a genre and assess examples of it, but also instills goals for writing in that genre.

If you have not already done so, distribute copies of the *Autobiography Web* on page 29. Have students discuss the web and amend it with their own ideas. Then ask students to work in groups of five or six to read an autobiography together. (See the *Annotated Bibliography*, page 104, for suggested titles.) Students can read chapters silently, or aloud to one another. After reading each chunk, students can discuss how well the author is fulfilling the criteria. After students have read the entire autobiography, provide groups with a chart to summarize their overall opinion about it. Suggest that the group appoint a spokesperson to present the autobiography critique to the class; and/or display group charts and suggest that students refer to them when choosing an autobiography to read independently.

2. *Plan and Carry Out Partner-Interviews* Informally reviewing highlights of one's life with a classmate is a pre-writing strategy that serves most students well. For reluctant writers or for those who feel they have "nothing interesting to tell" about their lives, the strategy can help uncover interesting information and build motivation and self-confidence. For all writers, considering and answering interview questions helps develop a focus or theme for an autobiographical piece.

Start by asking the class as a whole to contribute several interview questions under the following categories. Write their ideas on the board.

Facts About You. What is your name? How old are you? Where and when were you born? Do you live in an apartment or in a house? What is your address?

Family Facts. What are your parents' names? Where were they born? Do you have brothers and sisters? If so, what are their names and ages? Does anyone live with you besides your parents, brothers, and sisters? If so, who are they? Do you have pets? What are they? What are their names?

Note that the categories above call for straightforward information. For some students, this may be all they wish to share. Other students will wish to get into discussions of significant people and events which lie at the heart of autobiographical material.

Home and Neighborhood. What chores do you do around your home? What funny or odd things have happened while you did the chores? What special times do you celebrate or enjoy with your family? Do you remember something special about a particular family holiday, vacation, or special event? Who is your best friend in the neighborhood? Why do you like this person? What do you do together? What adventures have you shared?

School Days. What do you remember about your first year in school? What is the happiest thing that has happened to you in school? the saddest thing? What teacher or other adult at school has made the greatest impression on you? Why?

Other categories for which students can develop sample questions are *My Goals for the Future, Favorite Possessions, My Heroes, Significant Events.*

After brainstorming has wound-down, have students choose an interview partner. Explain that partners will take turns interviewing one another. The interviewer will ask his or her partner questions based on the class list, and record them via written notes and/or a tape recorder. Notes and tapes then go to the interviewee, who can use them as a resource when writing an autobiographical piece.

Conclude this step by bringing the class together to respond to these questions: (a) When you were being interviewed, what did you learn about yourself? (b) When you were the interviewer, did you get to know your partner better? Why or why not?

3. *Write an Autobiographical Incident* In an autobiographical incident, the writer narrates a personal experience that has made a lasting impression. The writing steps are as follows:

Identify the Incident Students who have participated in the partner interview described above may have already identified a significant personal event they wish to write about. For students who need more prompts, suggest the following sentence starters:

   ✳ I'll never forget the time when . . . .

   ✳ The biggest surprise of my life was when . . .

   ✳ The time when I felt proudest (happiest, saddest, most puzzled, etc.) was when . . .

Write a Focus Statement Ask students to summarize <u>why</u> the incident is important to them. Ask students to use this statement to guide their writing. *Examples:*

The incident is important to me because . . . .

   ✳ I learned that hard work pays off.

* I learned that an enemy can become a friend.

* I found out how much my grandfather is like me.

* I discovered a whole new interest in life.

Use Vivid Details in the Draft Remind students to describe the setting and the people in their autobiographical incident in detail. As practice, you might invite the class to expand simple statements with descriptive words, phrases, and sentences. *Examples:*

* I walked down the street.
  Lonely and sad, I walked down the empty street.

* Aunt Selma laughed.
  Aunt Selma laughed in that shy way she has, covering her mouth.

* Louie and I swam.
  Louie and I swam in the lake like two happy ducklings.

Conference and Revise Writing partners should use the following criteria as they assess one another's drafts and make suggestions for revising:

* The incident is identified and explained clearly.

* Vivid details describe the actions and people involved.

* The writer makes clear why this autobiographical incident is important to him or her.

Publish Some students may wish to keep their edited autobiographical incidents in their personal journal, or make it a part of their personal portfolio. Other students may elect to share their autobiographical work with classmates via a class Autobiography Anthology, an oral Autobiography Day, or a cooperative mural illustrating and captioning big events in their individual lives. Whatever mode individual students choose, help them summarize their experience of writing in this genre.

Some questions for discussion:

* What's fun about writing an autobiography?

* What's painful or difficult about writing an autobiography?

* Now that you've had some experience in writing your own autobiography, what will you look for when you read other people's autobiographies? (*Examples:* vivid descriptions; revelation of feelings; clear indications of why certain incidents or people are important to the writer.)

You may wish to conclude this activity by having students revisit the autobiographies they studied at the beginning of the unit to assess them anew.

4. *Use Your Life-Experience in Other Things You Write* Help students understand how their own life experiences enrich their writing in other genres. Ask partners to share their portfolios or journals to find entries that contain an autobiographical element. *Examples:*

✳ a poem in which you tell about how <u>you</u> sensed things, that is, about what you saw, heard, touched, and thought

✳ a first-hand biography that includes <u>your</u> reaction to a person you know well

✳ a folktale or fairy tale based on <u>your</u> memories of tales you heard or read long ago

✳ a realistic fiction story in which you adapted ideas and events from <u>your</u> life

✳ a science report in which you included what <u>you</u> observed and what <u>you</u> concluded

5. *Try the Autobiographical, or First-Person, Point of View in Different Kinds of Writing*
Invite students to use the first-person point of view when writing poems, stories, or reports about people from history, animals, or plants. For example, students might

✳ reread the poem on page 12, then write a poem in which the baby bat or the mother bat writes about the experience, using first-person pronouns;

✳ retell a fairy tale from the point of view of one of the characters in it—for example, from the viewpoint of the frog in "The Princess and the Frog";

✳ collect information about Harriet Tubman, then write a first-person journal entry in which Tubman tells about a rescue operation;

✳ report on the life cycle of a butterfly by taking the first person point of view, starting with the egg or larva.

CHAPTER 4

Reports of Information

TEACHER OVERVIEW

As readers, students encounter examples of this category in news stories, feature articles, nonfiction books on specific subjects, and articles in encyclopedias and special reference books. As writers, students know this category well, because they're so often assigned to write informational reports on a variety of subjects.

If your students have already explored biography and autobiography, they have some experience in reading for, critiquing and using factual data. However, in those literary categories, the data is usually arranged narratively, to tell a story of a life. In contrast, in most reports of information, data is organized conceptually, that is, around a central, controlling idea.

Focuses on a specific subject, or controlling idea

Organizes facts in a way that helps the audience learn about the subject

REPORT OF INFORMATION

Supports the controlling idea with plenty of facts

Uses examples, explanations, and descriptions to clarify ideas that may be new to the audience

PRE-READING ACTIVITIES

1. Writers and Subjects

Use a brainstorming activity to help students review how the same subject-matter may be used in a variety of literary genres. At the center of a chalkboard web, identify a subject that is of high interest to the class. Then have students suggest how ideas on that subject might be used in different kinds of literature. *Example:*

Poetry: word-pictures that tell about wolf cubs at night

Journal or diary: a real-life anecdote about the writer hearing wolves howl

WOLVES

Folktale: an old, make-believe tale in which a wolf is a main character

Historical fiction: a book about a pioneer family and its encounter with a wolf family

Realistic fiction: a novel about a girl who makes friends with a wolf

Science fiction or fantasy: a story about a planet where wolves are the rulers

Biography or Autobiography: the life story of a naturalist who studied wolves in their natural habitat

When the web is complete, present the class with this situation: Suppose you are asked to write a science report about wolves. What kinds of literature in the wolf web will be most useful to you? Why? (Answers will vary, but most students will choose journals, diaries, biography, and autobiography because these accounts are most likely to supply facts that a science report about wolves requires.)

Conclude the activity with this prompt: There's a kind of writing that is <u>not</u> included in the wolf web, but which would be very useful in finding facts for a science report about wolves.

This kind of writing is called *a report of information*. You can find reports of information in general encyclopedias like *World Book*. Where else can you find them?

Help students develop a rough list that includes specialized encyclopedias and dictionaries dealing with animals or wildlife, nonfiction trade books, articles in newspapers and magazines, and brochures and publications of environmental and regional groups. Students may also cite Internet resources, CD-ROMs, and TV programs and videotapes as sources of information.

2. Developing Criteria for Reports of Information

As a class, brainstorm possible characteristics of a report of information. Ask students to listen carefully to their classmates' suggestions so that they don't repeat them. Keep a list of students' suggestions to display later. Suggestions may range from the general to the specific. *Examples:*

* The report should be interesting.

* The report should supply a lot of important facts.

* The report should be up-to-date.

* The writer should explain difficult ideas. There should be descriptions, illustrations, and maps that help me understand what's being described.

* I like to know how the writer got the facts. Is it first-hand information, or does it come from what other people saw and did?

* I like when there is a main idea I can focus on.

When the brainstorming has wound-down, display the list of student suggestions, and distribute copies of the *Report of Information Web* on page 41. Invite students to link their criteria to specific sections of the web.

READING AND RESPONDING

1. Distribute copies of the excerpt on pages 44–45, which is from George Ancona's book *Powwow*. Explain that a powwow is a gathering of many Native American groups, who display and share their traditional music and dance. Ancona, a professional photographer and writer, collected powwow facts by attending the Crow Fair in Montana, which is the largest powwow held in the United States.

2. Distribute the *Powwow* **Response Guide** and review it with the class. Ask students to work with a partner or in small groups to read the excerpt together and write their responses.

Powwow

by George Ancona

Under the shade of the dancing arbor, the drums assemble. At a powwow, a group of singers who sing as they beat a rhythm in unison on a large drum is called a *drum*.

These singers must know many kinds of songs for all the different dances, honorings, and special events that can take place. The drums become the pulse and heartbeat of the powwow. The master of ceremonies will call upon each of the twenty-eight drums that are attending the fair to take turns singing for the dancers.

Good drums can become very popular. Fans and spectators cluster around their favorites to record the songs. They will use these recordings later to practice their own dancing and singing.

During breaks, the drum itself is covered with a blanket as a sign of respect.

Outside the dancing arbor, the dancers gather in a kaleidoscope of feathers, beadwork, fringe, and face paint. Inside the arbor, spectators find seats and wait for the dancing to begin. A feeling of excitement and anticipation fills the air. Everyone waits for the opening ceremony, called the Grand Entry, that signals the beginning of the dancing. The dancers form into groups according to the style of dance they will perform. Men, women, and children of all ages are dressed in one of the four dance categories: Traditional, Fancy, Grass, and Jingle-dress . . .

The first to dance are the Traditional men. Years ago, Native Americans lived close to nature, and this is reflected in the Traditional dancer's clothes. Feathers from eagles and other birds, porcupine quills, shells, horsehair, and the skins from deer, ermine, otter, wolf, and other animals are worn.

Traditional men wear a single bustle tied to the lower back. Some wear feathered bonnets, while others wear a warrior's hairpiece, called a roach,

made from deer tail, porcupine, or horsehair with one or two feathers in the center. They carry decorated weapons, feather fans, staffs, or other items that hold special meaning for the dancer. Some dancers also paint their faces in designs that reflect a personal vision. These designs can come from a dream or an important experience the dancer has had.

The Native Americans who lived on the Plains survived by hunting. The animals' flesh was used for food, skins became clothing, sinew became thread for sewing, and antlers and bones were made into tools. It was believed that the only way animals could be hunted and killed was if they understood the hunter's need and willingly gave themselves up to him. And if their gift of life was not respected, the next time the hunter went out, the animals would hide. Because of this relationship and dependence on nature, dancers honor the spirits of the animals that are part of their dance clothes. They treat their clothes with respect and care.

Powwow

RESPONSE GUIDE

Readers' names: _____ _____

1. In your own words, tell what you think the main idea of this excerpt is.

_____

_____

_____

2. Do you think the writer knows his subject well? Explain your answer.

_____

_____

_____

3. What new terms or phrases does Ancona help you understand? _____

_____

_____

How does he do that? _____

_____

_____

4. Copy some phrases or sentences from the excerpt that help you visualize or understand what is going on at the powwow. _____

_____

_____

_____

5. After Ancona describes Traditional Dancers, what do you think he will describe next?

_____

_____

Why do you think so? _____

_____

_____

Responding Options

1. Compare and Discuss Responses Work as a mentor as groups of students compare and discuss their responses. Though responses will vary, students should be expected to support them all with examples from the text. Overall, you may wish to stress and give particular support to the following ideas as they develop, and help students verbalize them:

✳ The report of information has a controlling idea, e.g., Native Americans gather to perform particular kinds of music and dance or, the men's Traditional Dance is one of the kinds of dances done at the powwow.

✳ The writer supplies many precise, vivid details to help readers envision what the musicians and dancers are doing.

✳ The writer explains the meaning of familiar words that are used in a special way. (e.g., At a powwow, <u>drum</u> means "a group of musicians," as well as " a musical instrument.")

✳ The writer has organized his facts. For example, he names the four dance categories (paragraph 5). Then he goes on to describe the first category (Traditional Dancers). Careful readers will correctly predict that Ancona will next describe Fancy Dancers, then Grass Dancers, then Jingle-dress Dancers.

You might conclude group discussions by focusing on what good reports of information share with other genres: the writer's enthusiasm for the subject; a clear presentation of ideas; or vivid details.

2. Evaluate the Excerpt Invite students to answer the question: "What else would you like to know about powwows?" Encourage a lot of lateral, divergent thinking, and enter students ideas on a chalkboard list. Examples:

✳ When did the idea of a powwow begin?

✳ What does the word <u>powwow</u> mean?

✳ Can people who are not Native Americans attend a powwow?

✳ What do kids do at a powwow?

✳ How are powwow dances like dances that other Americans do?

✳ How are powwows like other festivals in our country?

✳ In what way do Traditional Dancers at a powwow reflect my own ideas about the environment?

Move on from these subject-discrete questions to a larger, summarizing question: Why is Ancona's writing a fine example of a report of information? Suggest that students refer to their copies of the web on page 41 to develop their own answers to this question.

SYNTHESIZING AND APPLYING

1. Study Examples of Reports of Information Have students with common interests work in groups of five or six to locate, read, and critique at least three informational reports on their subject. Groups might develop a chart to present their critiques to classmates. *Example:*

Our Subject: The Habits of Wolves				
Name of Report	**Controlling Idea**	**Organization**	**Details**	**Explanation of New Ideas**
The Moon of the Gray Wolves, by Jean Craighead George	Arctic wolves have a hard time surviving.	A year in the life of a Gray Wolf	Many, especially about how wolf cubs are born and raised	Good job of explaining how wolves choose leaders.
Article, "Wolf," in *World Book Encyclopedia*	General survey of all kinds of wolves	The body of a wolf; the life of a wolf; wolves and people	Details about all the things in the organization column	There were some new terms, like "subordinate" and "hierarchy" that weren't made clear to us.

2. Evaluate Informational Reports About Current Events Students can use their insights about the components of good informational reports to build their awareness of current events. First, have students use common interests to form inquiry groups. Next, ask group members to develop questions they'd like to have answered on their chosen topic.

Explain that the group will essentially be constructing <u>A Report About Reports</u>. The task is to critique informational reports on your subject. Suggest the following steps:

✳ List your questions. Search through printed materials, visuals, and Internet resources to find the answers.

* Note each informational report you explore. If the report answered your question to your satisfaction, note the answer. If the report didn't answer the question satisfactorily, explain <u>why</u> it didn't.

* Suggest some ways in which a reporter might find answers to the unanswered questions. Usually students will not be able to carry out such inquiries themselves, but can discuss how intrepid professional reporters, in their quest for facts, often interview controversial persons, visit dangerous areas, and demand answers to "hot" questions.

While doing this activity you may wish to emphasize that because facts are always unfolding and coming to light, few informational reports tell "everything," and that reporters get information from many sources and are always seeking data that is most up-to-date and accurate. Suggest that students with strong reading skills read a national newspaper or news magazine to note the different sources the writer used to construct a report of information.

3. *Write a Report of Information* Take a break from curriculum-related topics, and have students brainstorm wide subjects of interest, such as <u>sports</u>, <u>animals</u>, <u>food</u>, or <u>movies</u>. Use the wide topic as the hub of a web, then encourage students to suggest subtopics that they could research and write about in a week's time. *Example:*

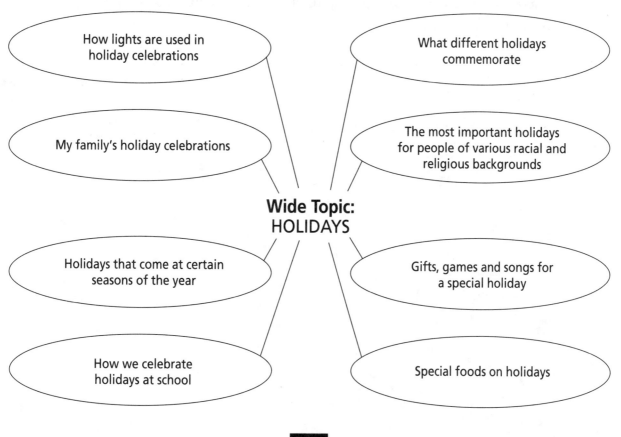

How lights are used in holiday celebrations

What different holidays commemorate

My family's holiday celebrations

The most important holidays for people of various racial and religious backgrounds

Wide Topic:
HOLIDAYS

Holidays that come at certain seasons of the year

Gifts, games and songs for a special holiday

How we celebrate holidays at school

Special foods on holidays

You may find it useful to make several webs like this, which revolve around several wide topics. Then have students follow with these steps:

* *Choose a subtopic.* This will be the controlling idea in your report. Write a controlling-idea statement. *Examples:* (1) Around the world, on almost every holiday, people use lights in special ways. (2) No matter who you are, you probably expect certain special dishes and foods at holiday times.

* *Think about the purpose of your report:* to give information accurately and effectively.

* *Think about your audience.* It will probably be your classmates and your teacher. What do they already know? What can you tell them that will be new and interesting to them?

* *Gather your facts and make notes.* Use a variety of sources including your own real-life experiences. Make sure all your facts relate to your controlling idea.

* *Draft your report.* In your draft, add descriptions and explanations that will help your readers visualize and understand what is happening.

* *Work with a writing partner to revise and edit your report.* Refer to the *Report of Information Web* to be sure that your drafts contain the characteristics of a good report of information.

CHAPTER 5

Fiction

Realistic Fiction in a Modern Setting

TEACHER OVERVIEW

Realistic fiction comes in two subgenres: (1) fiction in a modern setting, and (2) historical fiction. These subgenres naturally share major characteristics so you may wish to take them up sequentially, or even concurrently. (Compare this web with the *Historical Fiction Web* on page 61.)

 Characters: presents fictional characters who behave in realistic ways

 Setting: takes place in modern times; a recognizable sort of place

Realistic Fiction in a Modern Setting

A problem to solve: The main characters are involved in a conflict or dilemma.

Plot: has a plot that makes sense and that ends with the solution to the problem

Description: Places, events and characters are vividly described.

Dialogue: The characters' words show their personalities and also move the plot along.

PRE-READING ACTIVITIES

1. A "Reality Check"

You can use this activity to help students review what they already know about literary genres and to set the stage for an exploration of realistic fiction.

Supply the class with books and/or a list of titles that most of your students are familiar with. Make sure you present titles representing several different genres. (You may want to use the *Annotated Bibliography*, page 106 for ideas.)

Ask students to work in groups of four or five, and give each group a copy of the following chart. Ask the group to spend 10 to 15 minutes writing several titles that are examples of each chart heading. You may want to preview the chart and give some examples. Remind groups that they'll eventually be asked to support their choices with concrete evidence.

How Real?		
It really happened! **(Nonfiction)**	**It <u>could</u> happen.** **(Realistic fiction)**	**It <u>could</u> never happen!** **(Fantasy)**
A River Ran Wild	*Shoeshine Girl*	*A Ride on the Red Mare's Back*

Note: If your students have had little experience with classifying literature according to genre, you may want to preface the activity by discussing your own responses and the reasoning behind them.

For example:

Column 1, It really happened!: "To me, 'It really happened' means an event from history or current news. I think *A River Ran Wild* belongs in this category for the following reasons: the book tells about an actual New England river, gives facts about how it became polluted, and gives details about how real-life people cleaned it up. Because all the things in this book really happened, I think it is an example of **nonfiction**."

Column 3, It could never happen!: "I like the excitement in *A Ride on the Red Mare's Back*. And I admire the courage of the heroine. But I know this story is fictional, because there are no such things as trolls, and in real life a toy horse can't become a real horse. Because so much of the

story is make-believe and could never happen in real life, it is a **fantasy**."

Column 2, It could happen.: "I know that the writer, Clyde Bulla, made up the story *Shoeshine Girl*. He created the characters—Sarah Ida, Al, and Aunt Claudia—and he made up the town, Palmville. So, these characters and this place are **fictional**. But they seem very, very real! Sarah Ida does things that remind me of myself when I was young. Palmville seems like many towns I've visited, and all the events in the story seem quite possible. So I would call *Shoeshine Girl* **realistic fiction**: though the story is made up, it seems like something that could really happen."

Call on group spokespersons to tell the class some titles they listed in columns 1 and 3. Make a master chart to represent all groups' input. Have students confirm their choices by discussing, developing, and applying criteria for the categories. *Examples:*

✴ Nonfiction tells about real events and real people.

✴ Fantasy tells about unrealistic events and about people who have extraordinary powers or make-believe adventures.

When students wind down their input for columns 1 and 3 of the master chart, invite groups to revise or add to their entries in those columns.

2. Zero in on Realistic Fiction

Direct class attention to column 2 (It <u>could</u> happen.) on the group charts, and enter some of the groups' suggestions on the master chart. Distribute copies of the genre web on page 51, and ask students to apply these criteria to the titles they've listed. Encourage students to use their own brainstorms to support their choices. Allow time for classmates to respond to each others' ideas and to expand upon them.

READING AND RESPONDING

This activity will help students set up dialogues, or book talks, about realistic fiction they've shared.

✴ Have students form groups of six to eight readers. Ask each group to choose a realistic fiction book to read together. You may wish to consult the *Annotated Bibliography*, page 106, for ideas.

✳ Have each group form partner teams of two or three. Distribute the **Realistic Fiction in a Modern Setting Response Guide** and preview the prompts and questions. Explain that partners will work on the guide together during and/or after a group reading of the book.

✳ Ask the group to decide on a reading strategy. For example: (1) take turns reading aloud to the group, chapter-by-chapter or section-by-section; (2) make silent-reading assignments, with each group member responsible for covering a certain part of the book by a certain day; (3) have partners read the book together either aloud or silently.

✳ Ask partners to discuss possible responses to the guide and then complete it.

Realistic Fiction in a Modern Setting
RESPONSE GUIDE

Partners' names: _____ _____

Title and Author of Our Group's Book: _____
_____

1. Who are the main characters? What most impresses you about them?
_____
_____
_____

2. What is realistic about the setting? _____
_____
_____
_____

3. What big problem do the characters have to solve? _____
_____
_____
_____

4. Do the problem and the solution seem true-to-life? Explain. _____
_____
_____

5. Give an example of a dialogue and a descriptive passage that are particularly vivid and realistic. _____
_____
_____
_____
_____
_____
_____
_____

Responding Options

1. Share Responses Partners can get together with other members of their group to share and compare their responses to questions 1–4.

A group chairperson can facilitate the dialogue by taking each question in turn and calling on partners to present their responses. After group discussion of different ideas, one student can use a master copy of the **Realistic Fiction in a Modern Setting Response Guide** to record the ideas.

2. Focus on Descriptions Suggest that partners read aloud to their group the dialogue and descriptive passages they've identified for question 5. Before the reading, partners should state <u>why</u> they think the passages are realistic.

3. Discuss the Benefits of Book Talks Conclude the activity by asking students to reflect on how sharing a book helps you understand the story better. After considering and noting their group's various responses, individual students can complete a chart like the following: (Examples are based on Jean Craighead George's *Julie of the Wolves*.)

Book Title: *Julie of the Wolves*		
Book Elements	**My First Ideas**	**How Our Book Talk Added to My First Ideas**
Character	I thought Julie was brave, but foolhardy.	I can see that a kid raised in the Arctic might see survival strategies that would never occur to <u>me</u>!
Plot	The idea that a person would have to run away to escape a marriage seemed really weird to me!	I can see that the way a person behaves has a lot to do with the culture she was brought up in.
Problem Solving	I believe that Julie had to make big compromises between modern and traditional ways.	Our book talk verified my first idea. Everyone in my group talked about how hard it is to make decisions.

Encourage students to name other realistic fiction books they'd like to read with classmates, and to tell what events or characters they'd like to focus on.

SYNTHESIZING AND APPLYING

1. Read Critically Together Invite students to work in groups of five or six to read and critique three realistic fiction books that are new to them. (See the *Annotated Bibliography*, page 106, for some suggested titles.) Encourage groups to choose books that seem to fall into a category. *Examples:* people and their pets, family problems, kids at school, books written by the same author, or books set in three different countries or cultures.

Ask groups to set critical standards, or criteria, for assessing the books they plan to read. Suggest that they refer to their **Response Guide,** the webs on pages 51 and 61, and ideas they've gathered from pre-reading and post-reading discussions.

Each group should present the class with an overview of each book and an assessment of it according to the group's criteria. Encourage groups to organize their findings in the form of a chart or a web. Groups can refine this chart for class presentation on a bulletin board, or use it to develop other kinds of class presentations such as

* a round-table discussion of the three books;

* a Readers' Theater presentation of some of the "best" parts of each book;

* written or oral reviews of individual books.

2. Read and Respond Independently You'll probably want to encourage your students not only to read realistic fiction with classmates, but also to read in this genre alone—that's the only way to create the irreplaceable, personal dialogue between a reader and a piece of literature. Keep each student's thinking style, reading level, and tastes in mind as you direct reading and/or hold follow-up student-teacher dialogues about books. The following chart suggests levels of comprehension and kinds of responses you can ask for from different students according to where they "are." (Examples are from *Drylongso*, by Virginia Hamilton.)

Ways of Responding to a Story

Kind of Response	Definition	Example
Narrative (Literal)	Literal retelling of the plot; naming of main characters	"The story is about a farm family and a drought." "Drylongso comes to Lindy's house." "Drylongso teaches Lindy's father how to plant crops."
Personal (Associative)	Statements about how the student felt while reading; statements expressing relationships to the characters or incidents	"I like Lindy, because she's funny." "Mamalou is always making food, so she reminds me of my grandma."
Prescriptive	Student's ideas about what characters "should" have done, or about what the student would have done in a character's circumstance	"I think Drylongso should have stayed with Lindy's family." "If I was Lindy, I would have followed Drylongso."
Interpretive	Predicitons; inferences; relating the story to something else; expressing the theme	"I think Drylongso's idea will help Lindy's father be a better farmer." "Drylongso came along just in time." "Drylongso reminds me of Sarah, in *Sarah Plain and Tall*."
Literary Judgment	Rating writing and illustrations; identifying the genre; pointing out effective literary devices; evaluating the work	"The story is full of suspense." "The illustrations add to the story." "The story is so realistic that I felt like I was there." "I like the way the characters talk." "I want my friends to read this book."

3. Encourage Students to Plan and Draft Their Own Realistic-Fiction Stories While realistic fiction is a favorite genre of many young readers, the same students often have difficulty <u>writing</u> in this genre. Students may experience quick, genuine success when writing folktales, biographies, autobiographies, and reports of information, because these genres tend to be

formulaic or episodic. Realistic fiction, on the other hand, requires a lot of original thought and advance planning.

Following are some planning strategies for you to present and discuss with the class, and for student partners to try. The visuals, which you might copy on the chalkboard, are brainstorming starters for students to build on.

STRATEGY A: Think about **main problems** in realistic fiction books you've read. Use them to create related problems your story might focus on.

Main Problems in Books We've Read	Possible Problems in Stories We Might Write
In *Shoeshine Girl*, Sarah Ida wants an allowance, but her aunt won't give her one.	The main character wants a puppy, but his parents won't buy him one.
In *The Star Fisher*, Joan wants to feel at home in a new town, but she feels left out and lonely.	The main character likes the new neighbor, but his old friends don't, so he doesn't know what to do.
In *Drylongso*, a family must find a way to take care of their farm.	A family must find a way to take care of an aging relative.

STRATEGY B. Think about a problem you or someone you know has. Imagine a fictional character with this problem. Come up with some ways the character might solve the problem.

Problem: The main character misses her father. She can't visit him, because he lives far away.

Possible Solutions		
She does odd jobs for a whole year so that she can save money for a plane ticket to where her dad lives.	She writes letters to her dad and puts notes under her mom's pillow. These convince her parents that she needs to be with her dad a lot.	She learns how to use the Internet, her dad can use it, too. Now they can visit every day.

Point out to students who have used *Strategy A* that they can now use *Strategy B* to consider ways the main character in their own story might solve his or her problem.

STRATEGY C: <u>Choose a favorite folktale or fairy tale. Plan a way to update the story and make it realistic.</u>

Old Story: *Rumplestiltskin*	My Story: *Rodney Stilts*
Characters	
A miller's daughter A king A prince Rumplestiltskin	A cook's daughter A rich man The rich man's son Rodney Stilts
Setting	
A castle	A big mansion
Problem	
The miller's daughter has to guess Rumplestiltskin's name, or he will take her baby away.	The cook's daughter has to guess what Rodney Stilts put in the birthday sandwiches, or the rich man's son will have an allergy attack.

Students can continue the story-planning practice by brainstorming plot steps and ways to solve the problem.

4. Encourage Students to Critique Their Own Realistic Fiction Stories According to the Criteria for This Genre

As students work with partners to revise their stories, suggest that they use the web on page 51 to assess the story components. For example, students might ask

* Is the setting one that most readers can recognize?

* Are characters and events described vividly?

* Do the characters behave and speak in realistic ways?

* Is the central problem the main character must solve clear?

* Does each step in the plot make sense?

* Is the problem solved satisfactorily?

After revising and editing their stories, students can make copies for classmates, then adapt the suggested evaluation criteria in *Read Critically Together*, page 57.

CHAPTER 6

Historical Fiction

TEACHER OVERVIEW

Because historical fiction and modern realistic fiction share many characteristics, you may want your students to explore these two realistic fiction subgenres together or sequentially. Also, keep in mind that children and adults usually have different ideas about what "history" is, i.e. about what constitutes "long ago." For most middle-graders, stories set during or prior to World War II can qualify as historical fiction.

Characters: all may be fictional; or some may be real, while others are fictional; <u>they all behave in realistic ways</u>

Setting: a definite period in history; a real historical place

HISTORICAL FICTION

A problem to solve: The main characters are involved in a conflict or dilemma <u>that is realistic for that period</u>.

Plot: a plot that makes sense and ends with a solution to the problem; <u>real events are mixed with fictional events</u>

Description: Places, events and characters are vividly described. <u>The writer explains historical information that may be unfamiliar to readers.</u>

Dialogue: The characters' words show their personalities, move the plot along, and reflect what people knew and thought about in those times.

PRE-READING ACTIVITIES

1. Drawing on Prior Reading

In past years, through books like *Ox-Cart Man*, *The Biggest Bear*, and *Molly's Pilgrim*, most students have already enjoyed historical fiction, though they may not have learned the formal term or spent much time analyzing what's "historical" about the stories. Now, to help your students recognize the importance of <u>time</u> in historical and modern realistic fiction, copy and discuss the following chart, and have students suggest answers to the question at the bottom. (Some possible responses are given in parentheses.)

Realistic Fiction	
Drylongso	*Sarah, Plain and Tall*
Characters: a farm family / a newcomer *Place:* a farm *Time:* the 1970's	*Characters:* a farm family / a newcomer *Place:* a farm *Time:* the late 1800's
How does the time of the story affect the characters' lives?	
(Farmers have tractors with motors; airplanes are common; the land is getting worn out.)	(Farmers use horse-drawn plows; trains make slow trips; pioneers are clearing new land for growing crops.)

Ask students which book in the chart they would classify as <u>modern fiction</u>, and which as <u>historical fiction</u>. Have them support their responses, for example, "*Drylongso* is modern fiction, because it's set about 25 years ago; because it tells about things in the world today." "*Sarah, Plain and Tall* is historical because it's set about 100 years ago; a farm family's life was very different then."

Next, help students focus on what's <u>realistic</u> about both books. For example: the characters have problems that we can recognize as being like our own (making a living, missing a parent, getting acquainted with someone new); the characters act and talk in believable ways. The plots in both books are true-to-life: a newcomer (Drylongso) teaches lessons about wise farming; two children want a newcomer (Sarah) to be their new mother.

Conclude this pre-reading activity by asking students to work in small groups to list several books they agree are <u>historical fiction</u>. For this purpose, you may wish to have groups use the library, or skim realistic fiction books you have in your classroom collection. (See the *Annotated Bibliography*, page 107, for suggested titles.) Explain that groups should be able to support their choices now, but will have an opportunity to change their minds later on.

2. "Golden Oldies": Favorite Old Times and Places

In this activity, students identify a time and place they would like to have experienced first-hand. Explain that the activity will help students (a) zero in on historical fiction titles that represent their special interests; (b) synthesize ideas they've gleaned from their work in social studies and through their previous reading and viewing; (c) consider the kind and scope of information readers look for, and historical fiction writers try to gather, about particular periods of history. Then present an oral time machine tour like the one below:

> Close your eyes. The time machine won't work unless your eyes are shut tight. Okay, with a whir of machinery noises, you are traveling through time and space to the most wonderful, fascinating place way back in time that <u>you've</u> ever studied! *Remember:* It's a <u>real</u> place and time, not some make-believe, fantasy place. Maybe you've read about it, or seen a TV show or movie or CD-ROM version of it. Anyway, this place and time have always intrigued you . . . and there you are!

> You clamber out of the time machine. Look around. Whom do you see? <u>What</u> do you see? What are people doing? What do you hear? What puzzles you about these surroundings? Remember as many details as you can, so that you can tell about your observations when you return to the present . . . . Which is right <u>now</u>!

Ask students to quickly jot down notes about the place and time they envisioned. Then ask them to add questions they have about that setting. Questions may range from the everyday ("What did people eat back then?" "What did they do for a living?") to the philosophical ("What did they believe about the universe?"). Invite students to share some of their questions with the class and to tell where they might find answers to these questions (encyclopedias, nonfiction books,

Internet resources, etc.). Then distribute copies of the *Historical Fiction Web* on page 61. Discuss the web, asking students to point out which of their questions might be answered in a historical fiction book set in the era they envisioned.

READING AND RESPONDING

✳ Distribute copies of the excerpt from Elizabeth Janet Gray's *Adam of the Road*. Explain that this is the beginning of the first chapter of a historical fiction book: the setting is England about 500 years ago during the Middle Ages.

✳ Distribute the ***Adam of the Road* Response Guide**. Ask students to work with a partner or small group to preview the guide, read the selection, and complete the activity sheet.

Adam of the Road

by Elizabeth Janet Gray

After a May as gray and cold as December, June came in, that year of 1294, sunny and warm and full of birds and blossoms and all the other happy things the songs praise May for. Adam Quartermayne, who had been looking for his father ever since Easter, thought that now he would surely come. Every morning when he rolled out of his bed in the long dormitory where the school boys slept, he said to himself, "Today he's coming! I know it!" and every night, disappointed but not daunted, he put himself to sleep making up stories about how his father would come the next day.

Sometimes he made him come just at the end of choir practice, sometimes at the beginning of the lesson in grammar, sometimes in the middle of dinner when the boys ate their meat and pottage in silence while a master read aloud in Latin from the lives of the saints. However Adam's stories began, they all ended with Roger the minstrel taking Adam right out of school. Across the courtyard they would go striding, Adam with his own harp over his shoulder and his father's viol under his arm; through the gateway they would pass and over the river to the highway that led to London and all the wide, free world.

It was a famous school that the monks kept in the Abbey of St. Alban, but Adam had had enough of it. Five long months ago his father had left him there while he himself went to France, to the minstrels' school held in Lent each year at Cambrai, where he would learn new romances to tell to the lords and ladies of England.

Roger Quartermayne was no ordinary minstrel, picking up an uncertain penny telling rough yarns in inn-yards and market places, filling in gaps in his memory with juggling and tumbling and piping as the poorer sort did. He could play the viol; he could chant long romances in French about King Alisaunder, or Charlemagne and his knights, or the British King Arthur and the search for the Holy Grail. He was welcome at manor houses and at great feasts in castles, and everywhere people gave him rich gifts, a length of cloth for a surcoat, a purse full of silver pennies, or a gold clasp to fasten his mantle. He went attended by a boy to carry his viol and to sing with him when there were songs in the tales or harp a little in the interludes, and that boy, from his eighth birthday till his eleventh last February, had been Roger's son Adam.

So Adam watched eagerly for his father and talked endlessly about him to the other boys in school. He always spoke of him as Roger the minstrel, as if everyone must have heard of him, and if he was a little cocky about being the son of such a man, they forgave him. They liked Adam, because he was tousleheaded and snub-nosed, wide-mouthed and square-jawed, because his gray eyes were honest and twinkling, because he sang so well and knew so many stories, and because, though he boasted about Roger, he had a humble enough opinion of himself. They watched for Roger, too, and they all expected him, from Adam's description, to be as handsome as Earl Gilbert, who came sometimes to the abbey, but kinder, as brave as the king, but younger, and as grand as the abbot himself, but more comfortable.

Adam of the Road
RESPONSE GUIDE

Readers' names: _____   _____

1. **Facts:** The place is _____, the year is _____,
and the month is _____. The main character is _____.
He is living in a _____. His goal is _____
_____ .

2. What seems especially unfamiliar to you about the setting? _____
_____
_____
_____

3. In what way does Adam remind you of modern-day kids? _____
_____
_____
_____

4. List any words or phrases from the selection that are new to you. _____
_____
_____

In what ways might you find explanations of the words and phrases?
_____
_____
_____

5. Tell two things you'd hope to find out if you continued to read *Adam of the Road.*
_____
_____
_____
_____

Responding Options

1. *Share Responses* Students can work together with other partners or groups to compare and discuss their responses. Help students focus on answers to these questions:

* ✳ What makes this story <u>realistic</u>?

* ✳ What makes this story <u>historical</u>?

* ✳ What historical facts will the writer have to tell us so that we can understand and enjoy this story?

* ✳ How could this book add to our understanding of the Middle Ages?

A group spokesperson might present the group's ideas to the class for wider discussion and debate.

2. *Assess the Excerpt* Ask the class to use the web on page 61 to assess the excerpt from *Adam of the Road.* Accept all reasonable answers to the following sample questions, and encourage debate of responses that vary. Does Adam behave in a realistic way? How about his friends at school? Is the setting firmly established? Is there enough description to help you understand Adam's situation? If so, give some examples. Based on this excerpt, what do you think Adam will do as the story progresses? (Suggest that students use the book title and what they've read so far to make their predictions.)

3. *Relate the Excerpt to the Present Day* Invite volunteers to talk about modern situations that reflect what Adam is experiencing. *Examples:* having a hard time at school; missing an absent parent; having a special hobby, pet, or friend; admiring what a family member or close adult friend does for a living.

SYNTHESIZING AND APPLYING

1. *Reset the Story* To help students understand the <u>realism</u> in historical fiction, invite them to work with partners to rewrite the excerpt from *Adam of the Road* by changing the setting to "today." You may wish to provide a prompt:

Imagine that Adam is a modern-day kid who has been sent off to a boarding school, a summer camp, or a relative's home. Rewrite the story-starter, using as many ideas from the original as you can.

Encourage partners to share their rewrites with the class, then discuss how basic human situations and feelings hold true across the centuries.

2. *Play With Time-Incongruities* This listening/thinking exercise can help students look for time consistency when they read historical fiction, and also avoid incongruities when they write in that genre. Explain that you are going to read aloud a paragraph that inserts some modern facts into the medieval setting of the original. Ask students to listen carefully and note anything that Adam—in his thirteenth-century world—could not possibly have known about or done. (These are underlined in the passage.)

> Here it was, June in the year 1294, and Adam had not yet received the <u>express mail letter</u> his father had promised to send him. Adam was a student in a boarding school that taught trades such as <u>auto mechanics</u> and carpentry. He often felt stranded, because there was no way to reach his family by <u>telephone</u>. Adam's father was a musician, a master of the <u>electric guitar</u>. He traveled around the country <u>by plane</u>, and there was no way of predicting where he would be from week to week.

After students have identified the incongruous elements, you might write the paragraph on the chalkboard and ask partners to rewrite it to make it fit medieval days. You may also wish to point out what <u>does</u> remain consistent over the centuries, such as getting an education, making a living, and feeling attached to one's family.

3. *Encourage Student Groups to Read and Report on Historical Fiction Set in Specific Periods* Take an informal survey to find out about what places and periods of history students are interested in. *Examples:* Africa (or America) before the time of European exploration; Japan in the time of the samurai; the Caribbean and Central America before the time of the Spanish explorers; Polynesian explorers of the South Pacific; European explorers of the Americas; ancient Egypt; ancient Greece or Rome.

Invite students with similar historical interests to form groups and read two or three historical fiction books set in that era. (See the *Annotated Bibliography*, page 107 for suggested titles.) Groups might aim for a report to the class that addresses the criteria in the *Historical Fiction Web* on page 61. For follow-up class discussion, talk about how historical fiction adds to our understanding of how people behaved and thought long-ago.

4. *Invite Students to Write Historical-Fiction Anecdotes* Writing an entire, plotted fiction story that accurately renders a time period and real historical figures is a task beyond the writing maturity of most middle-grade students. However, after carrying out some of the earlier activities, most students can compose an anecdote or brief narrative, in which a fictional character modeled on themselves interacts with a real historical figure in an actual episode from history.

Explain the expected outcome of the activity. Then, to help implement such anecdotes, ask students to focus on a historical person whom they greatly admire. Have students research and note what they feel are the outstanding attributes and actions of the person they admire. *Example:*

> I admire Chief Joseph of the Nez Perce Indians. He loved his people's traditional lands, but grieved when he saw how warriors and their families died as they tried to protect it from U.S. soldiers. Chief Joseph had to make a choice: continue fighting, or surrender.

After students make these notes, ask them to imagine that they are friends or companions of the historical person they admire. Read aloud the following piece as an example of what students are to do.

> I am a young warrior of the Nez Perce, and my name is Wolf Calling. For many months I have followed Chief Joseph through the snowy mountains seeking to find a place where the white soldiers will leave us alone. As we approach Canada, the soldiers come near, and I raise my weapons. But my Chief says, "Put the weapons down."
>
> I obey, but I do not understand until I hear Joseph's next words: "Too many of my people have died already. I must look for their bodies. Perhaps I will find my own children among them. From this day forward, I will fight no more."
>
> As I lower my weapons, I think, " This is the end of my life as Wolf Calling, my life as a brave defender of my people. From now on, I am not a Call, but only an Echo of a vanished way of life"

Other real people that students might research and then incorporate into dramatic, historical fiction anecdotes are Harriet Tubman; Martin Luther King, Jr.; Christopher Columbus; Susan B. Anthony; Benjamin Franklin; Florence Nightingale; Louis Pasteur; and Sojourner Truth.

CHAPTER 7

Folk Literature

TEACHER OVERVIEW

Folk literature is made up of recorded legends, fairy tales, pourquoi (why-it-happened) tales, fables (moral stories), and trickster tales.

As a genre, folk literature has the following characteristics:

1
Usually does not have a single, identifiable author

2
Originates in oral tellings, and thus may appear in different versions in print

FOLK LITERATURE

3
Features stock characters who are either "all bad" or "all good"

4
Has fantastic or unrealistic elements in it

5
Usually has an easily discernible lesson or moral

6
Is set in a vague historical past "long ago"

PRE-READING ACTIVITIES

1. Oral Story-Telling

To help students capture the ambiance in which folk literature originates and is transmitted, set up a stories-without-books session. Have students sit in a circle. Ask them to imagine that books have temporarily disappeared from the world. How are people going to share stories they know and learn new ones? Most students will respond that people can tell stories aloud. Encourage students to identify different kinds of stories they might tell.

Some students may suggest telling true-life anecdotes. Others may suggest making up original fantasy stories. Remind students that in addition to these kinds of stories, they already have a vast mental library of stories that have been told aloud to them through the years. Use prompts and models such as the following to help students think of examples of such stories:

✳ I remember my grandmother telling me the story of the Gingerbread Boy. What's a make-believe story your family told you when you were very young?

✳ A lot of stories I remember have animal characters, like the story of the race between the tortoise and the hare. Do you remember any stories like that?

✳ I remember hearing many fairy tales when I was young. My favorite was (_____). What was your favorite fairy tale? Why did you like it?

Continue in this way with examples of pourquoi stories, such as how the leopard got his spots; legends, such as those about Davy Crockett; and trickster stories, such as those about Bre'r Rabbit and Bre'r Fox. Along the way, ask students to indicate whether a story a classmate recalls is familiar to them. As students begin to realize that they have a common stockpile of stories, introduce and explain the term *folk stories* (stories handed down generation after generation by word of mouth by the "folk": ordinary people). Explain that most folk stories are so old that nobody knows who first told them.

Conclude the activity by calling on volunteers to carry on the oral tradition by telling an old, familiar folk story aloud to the group. Ask the audience to listen and decide what <u>kind</u> of folk story it is (e.g., a fairy tale? fable? legend?), and why they enjoyed listening to it. If necessary, begin by modeling with your own oral retelling of a folk story.

2. Looking at the Literature

Explain that once a story is written down, it has become *literature*. Point out the separate books and anthologies of folk literature in your classroom collection. Ask students to work with a partner to find the following:

* examples of two of the different kinds of folk stories discussed in activity 1

* examples of folktales from different cultures

* different versions of the same story

* names of two writers or editors who have collected or retold folk stories

* titles of some folk stories that they would like to read thoroughly

Ask partners to discuss their responses with a larger group or with the class. Note key responses on the chalkboard or on poster paper for students to refer to in carrying out one of the *Synthesizing and Applying* activities.

READING AND RESPONDING

Ask partners to choose two folk stories to study closely.

Distribute the **Folk Literature Response Guide**. Ask partners to read together the two stories they have chosen, then use the guide to compare the stories and record their ideas and reactions.

Folk Literature
RESPONSE GUIDE

Partners' names: _____ _____

Title 1: _____ **Title 2:** _____

1. Describe the main characters:

_____ _____

_____ _____

_____ _____

_____ _____

_____ _____

2. What is the main problem the characters must solve?

_____ _____

_____ _____

_____ _____

3. What lessons do the characters learn?

_____ _____

_____ _____

_____ _____

_____ _____

_____ _____

4. What is unusual and fantastic about the story ?

_____ _____

_____ _____

_____ _____

_____ _____

5. What did you like best about the story and why?

_____ _____

_____ _____

_____ _____

_____ _____

Responding Options

1. Share Responses Individual responses will vary depending on what specific tales partners have chosen. However, the responses in general will reflect students' grasp of characteristics 3–6 of the genre as shown in the *Folk Literature Web* on page 71. Invite partners to share their responses with you and a group of classmates, and encourage reactions from any group member who is familiar with the story. Accept all responses that students can support with examples. Use varying responses and differences of opinion to spark lively discussions.

2. Identify and Explore Forms of Folk Literature Help students further develop their recognition of the different kinds of folk stories and their specific characteristics. Present each of the following descriptive prompts, then ask students to give examples from the stories they have just read and responded to. Invite one or two students to make a chalkboard chart to record story types, characteristics, and examples as classmates discuss them.

  ✳ <u>Fairy tales</u> are usually set in a vague time, "a long time ago." They feature make-believe people who have strange tasks or challenges to meet, and who are helped by magical, mysterious beings. (*Examples:* "The Frog Prince," "Cinderella")

  ✳ <u>Legends</u> are usually set in a recognizable place and time (e.g., the Great Plains before the coming of Europeans) and feature a human heroine or hero who performs super-human deeds. This heroic character is often based on a real, historical figure whose prowess has been exaggerated through time and retellings.

  ✳ <u>Fables</u> are very short tales and usually end with a moral that suggests a wise way of behaving, such as "Don't count your chickens until they're hatched." Some fables have human characters, but most star animals that act like humans. (*Examples:* "The Fox and the Grapes," "The Dog and the Bone," "The Milkmaid and Her Pail")

  ✳ <u>Pourquoi stories</u> are imaginative tales that tell why or how something in nature came to be that way. The characters are usually animals. (*Examples:* "Why Rabbit Has a Short Tail," "How Birds Got Their Colors")

  ✳ <u>Trickster Tales</u> star an animal—like Fox, Crow, Coyote or Anansi the Spider—who delights in deceiving other animals. The trickster usually wins, not only because of his cleverness, but also because of some character flaw of his victim, such as vanity or pride. (*Examples:* "Bre'r Rabbit, Bre'r Fox, and the Briar Bush," and "How Coyote Fooled Snake")

3. Recognize the Importance of the Oral Tradition Remind students again of the oral origins of folk stories and of how the stories were told and enjoyed by people of all ages. Invite students to suggest some reasons why both adults and children shared the stories. *Examples:*

✳ In the days before people had books or knew how to write, telling stories aloud was a way of preserving them through the years.

✳ Telling stories aloud was fun, as it is today.

✳ Most folktales state or hint at approved ways of behaving, such as being honest or working hard. The stories were a way of teaching these values to children and reinforcing them for adults.

SYNTHESIZING AND APPLYING

1. Encourage Students to Use Folktale Formats for Their Own Stories Ask students to refer to the chart their classmates have made for Responding Option 2, and choose the kind of folktale they'd like to write on their own. The stories can be entirely new, or can be modern adaptations of a traditional tale. Students may wish to work independently or with a writing partner. You might suggest these strategies to help students get started:

✳ If you're writing a fable or a pourquoi story, decide ahead of time what your story will teach or explain.

✳ If you're writing a fairy tale, decide ahead of time who the "good" and "bad" characters will be, what task the good character must perform, and what magic will help him or her perform it.

✳ If you're writing a trickster tale, decide ahead of time which animal will be the trickster, which animal will be the victim of the trick, and what the victim will learn through his or her encounter with the trickster.

✳ If you're writing a legend, decide what real-life person you'll use as a main character, and what unusual strengths or super powers this hero or heroine will have.

Suggest that students use visual devices to plan their stories. You might present the following as examples:

Story Steps (*Example:* a Fable)
Title: The Moth and the Eagle
The moral: Be satisfied with who you are.

6. Moth learns to be
happy with who he is.

5. Moth burns
his wings.

4. Moth flies too
near the sun.

3. Eagle challenges
Moth to prove it.

2. Moth says he can
fly as high as Eagle.

1. Moth is jealous
of Eagle.

Story Web (*Example:* a fairy tale)

Characters:
• a good prince
• an evil prince
• a mysterious princess

Situation:
The bad prince has captured the good prince and princess. He has imprisoned them in separate towers.

Title: <u>The Prisoner Prince</u>

Setting:
A faraway land long ago

Problem:
The good prince wants to escape.

Main Actions

1. From her tower window, the princess shows the prince a feather and a handful of hay. She says he has three guesses about what they stand for. If he guesses correctly, both he and she will be free.

2. The prince makes three wrong guesses! The princess starts to cry.

3. Her tears make her melt, then she changes her shape. She turns into a flying horse.

4. The horse flies to the prince's tower and rescues him.

5. The good prince is free now, and the horse is, too. It had been changed into a princess by the evil prince.

After students have held writing conferences and revised and edited their stories, invite volunteers to read or tell their stories aloud to a group of classmates. Ask the audience to listen to determine what kind of folk story it is (e.g., a legend, a pourquoi story) and why they think so.

Note: Students in the middle grades sometimes write folk stories that combine characteristics of folk literature. For example, a fairy tale may have a fable-like moral to it; a pourquoi story may have some characteristics of a legend. In student writing, don't insist on strict adherence to type in every detail.

2. ***Suggest Different Ways of Publishing and Sharing Original Folktales***

✹ An illustrated book for each story. Partners can read and discuss, and then illustrate and bind one another's folk tales.

✹ A class anthology. Students can organize their stories according to type, then appoint groups of classmates to (1) write an introduction for each type; (2) write brief bios of each student author; (3) number pages and make a table of contents; (4) design and illustrate a cover for the anthology.

✹ Sharing with other classes. Your students can display their separate books or class anthology in the school library, and discuss with the librarian ways to get other classes involved in enjoying the anthology and in using it as a stepping-stone to their own study of folk literature.

Some of your students may also enjoy telling or reading their original tales to younger children in your school, then inviting the audience to illustrate the stories.

✹ Sharing with families. Students can work together to compose a letter to family members to tell what the class has learned about folk literature. Make a copy of the letter for each student, and suggest that the student attach it to a copy of his or her original folk story.

3. ***Translate Folk Literature Into Other Media*** Students can work in cooperative groups to plan and carry out additional ways of sharing folk stories. Possibilities to consider:

✹ Staged dramatizations of their original tales, or of key events in them, or of traditional folk stories. Some students may enjoy presenting these as pantomimes and asking the audience to guess the story title.

✹ "Radio plays," or taped dramatizations of stories; later—individually or with a partner—students can listen as they follow along with a printed version to enjoy their classmates' renditions.

✹ <u>Draw picture-panels, with dialogue balloons,</u> showing the main events in a favorite folktale to collect in a "Folk Comics" book or post on a bulletin board.

✹ <u>Stage a class quiz show</u> with teams taking turns writing and presenting questions based on folk stories—old and original—that they have enjoyed together. Suggest that students think up special prizes to award to winners, such as slips of paper labeled "You get three wishes," "You get to kiss a toad," or "You out-tricked the trickster!"

✹ <u>Create a mural</u> showing characters and exciting events from favorite folktales.

✹ <u>Write songs about folk story heroines and heroes,</u> with original lyrics, set to the tune of existing or original melodies; students can tape-record their songs, or present them "live" to the class.

4. *Find and Share Folktales From a Variety of Cultures* Students can explore folk literature representing their own heritage or a culture they are studying in your classroom. See the *Annotated Bibliography*, pages 107–109, for sources students might use. Alert your librarian to the project. Many students may also have resource people at home or in the neighborhood who can tell them culture-specific stories. Encourage students to tell the stories aloud to classmates. As a follow-up activity, discuss with students how the stories are alike and how they are different.

5. *Make Folk Stories a Part of Your Read-Aloud Agenda* Once or twice a month, read or tell a folk story to the class. After eliciting general reactions as a way to review this genre, help students focus on qualities that the story shares with other literary genres, for example: exciting plots, strong characters, themes and messages, vivid descriptions, effective dialogue, and sensory language.

CHAPTER 8

Mystery

TEACHER OVERVIEW

The mystery story has the components of other realistic fiction, but with a vital change of emphasis: everything in the story revolves around a puzzle, or an unusual problem to solve, as delineated in this web:

Characters: all involved in the basic problem to solve, or puzzle

Setting: realistic

MYSTERY: A PROBLEM TO SOLVE
Who did it? What is it? How did it happen?

Clues: The writer drops hints that *might* help the reader solve the mystery.

Distractions: Some things in the story are meant to distract readers, that is, to lead them away from the solution.

Plot: Each major event is linked in steps that make sense.

Conclusion: The story ends with a credible, realistic solution to the mystery.

PRE-READING ACTIVITIES

1. Mysteries as Riddles

Since so many kids love riddles, you might introduce your students' study of mysteries by presenting and discussing this riddle/problem:

> A boy is hurt in a bicycle accident. The ambulance driver rushes the boy to a hospital and calls the child's father, Dr. Smith. Dr. Smith meets the ambulance at the emergency room and becomes hysterical when he sees his injured son. In the operating room, where the boy is taken for surgery, Dr. Smith gazes into the child's face, then says, "I'm glad this is not my son!"

In this classic riddle, the puzzle is explained by the fact that there are <u>two</u> Dr. Smith's: one is the father, and the other is the surgeon. Kids may or may not figure this out. The important point for you to make is that the riddle, or mystery, for the reader is based on <u>mistaken identity</u>. In less blatant forms, mistaken or confused identity is at the core of many mysteries, and is the twist this chapter concentrates on, mainly because it's the easiest focus for young writers to use when constructing their own mystery stories.

2. Drawing on Previous Reading: Identities and Clues

Invite the class to discuss mystery stories they have enjoyed recently. Students may first mention examples from TV, computer games, or movies. *Ask:* What is the problem that had to be solved? Who were the "suspects"? What were the clues that lead you to suspect more than one character? Did you guess the correct solution before you reached the end of the story? Looking back at the plot, does the solution make sense? Why, or why not?

Ask similar questions about mystery stories in books that students are likely to be familiar with, such as one of Donald Sobel's *Encyclopedia Brown* adventures. For example, in Sobel's *The Case of the Missing Ring*, clues about the typewriter and about Mr. Bevan's cane are given early-on in the story. Discuss how a reader, looking back, can see how these clues were "planted" by the writer to help identify the perpetrator; and how, unless one picked up on these clues, many other characters in the story might be suspected as the thief.

3. What's Fun About Mysteries?

Invite the class to brainstorm answers to this question from both the reader's and the writer's point of view. *Examples:*

✳ From the reader's point of view, it's fun
   . . . getting into the excitement of an unsolved problem;
   . . . trying to figure out "who did what;"
   . . . trying to guess the solution to the mystery.

✳ From the writer's point of view, it's fun
   . . . setting up a situation that will keep your readers curious and excited;
   . . . planning how the situation will turn out in a logical, believable way;
   . . . planting small clues along the way to help careful readers follow along as you finally answer mysterious questions.

READING AND RESPONDING

Although Patricia C. McKissack's short mystery story "The Chicken-Coop Monster" doesn't deal with crimes, detectives, and nefarious perpetrators, it has the essential characteristics of a mystery: an ominous problem to be solved; a realistic setting; a main character (in this story, the first-person narrator) who is pulled into solving the mystery. For learning and instructional purposes, the story provides a fine, doable model for young writers who want to tackle the mystery genre, because it's based on a universal, familiar recollection: "something-that-scared-me-when-I-was-little-kid." The beginning of McKissack's story is provided here.

Ask students to form reading/response groups of four or five. Give a copy of the excerpt and **The Chicken-Coop Monster Response Guide** to each student. Ask groups to read the excerpt together, pencil-in their individual responses, then discuss and compare responses, changing them if they wish to do so.

The Chicken-Coop Monster

by Patricia McKissack

The year I turned nine, my parents' ten-year marriage ended in divorce. The grownups never talked about it around me, but I knew what was going on. Mama and Daddy didn't love each other anymore. So where'd that leave me?

As soon as school was out, they shipped me off to the Tennessee boonies to stay with my grandparents, Franky and James Leon Russell. I didn't want to go, but no one was listening to me.

A monster lived there. I knew it the minute I set foot on their farm. I was president of the St. Louis chapter of the Monster Watchers of America, and I was an expert on spotting monsters.

It lived in the chicken coop—the tingling on the back of my neck was strongest when I passed by there. Its hot, mean eyes watched me as I played on the back porch. Sometimes I chased my ball too close and smelled its foul breath. This wasn't an ordinary in-the-closet fright or an under-the-bed scare. I'd come upon something really terrible.

I needed help with this one, so I wrote to my friend Jay, who was in charge of the MWA over the summer. Jay and I had been best buddies since we'd started the MWA the year before. By enclosing fifty cents and six box tops from Crinkle cereal, we'd sent away for and received an official MWA Club starter kit, complete with six badges, six glow-in-the-dark ID cards, and a manual containing ten monster rules and everything else we needed to know about creepy stuff. We'd invited Nora, Jeff, Latisha, and Alandro to join us.

Writing to Jay made me feel better. Meanwhile, I had to be careful not to break any monster rules, because that would make the thing stronger and bolder.

One evening Ma Franky called me to the kitchen. "Missy, I forgot to throw the latch on the chicken coop. Go lock it for me, please."

The sun had set, but there was a little light left in the sky. The backyard was already engulfed by a blanket of darkness, but I could see the silhouette of the old chicken shack against the sky.

I stood on the back porch, a statue of fear. This is what the monster had been waiting for. I heard the whisper of its tail swishing in the straw.

The Chicken-Coop Monster

RESPONSE GUIDE

Name: _____

Think About Facts:

1. Where is the narrator living as the story begins? _____
Why is she living there? _____
_____
_____

2. Why is the narrator afraid of the chicken coop? What reasons does she give for her
fear? _____
_____
_____

Think About Feelings:

3. What is the narrator upset about? List at least <u>two</u> examples. _____
_____
_____
_____

4. Circle words and phrases in the story that describe the narrator's feelings well.

Predict:

5. What do you think the chicken-coop monster is? _____
Why do you think so? _____
_____
_____
_____

6. In your opinion, how can the narrator solve the mystery of the chicken-coop monster?
_____
_____
_____

Responding Options

1. **Share Responses** Bring groups together to discuss their responses to the beginning of McKissack's story. Most students will generally agree on responses to questions 1–3. (She is living on her grandparents farm because her parents are getting divorced. She is afraid of the chicken coop because she thinks there is a monster in it. As the president of the St. Louis chapter of the Monster Watchers of America, she knows a lot about monsters. She is upset by her parents divorce and by the fact that she had no say in where she was going to spend the summer.)

Responses to question 4 may vary. Be sure to ask students to explain why they felt the words and phrases they circled were particularly descriptive.

2. **Encourage Divergent Ideas** You might set up a chalkboard chart like the one that follows to record varying responses to the prediction questions on the **Response Guide**. Then students might discuss

✳ how their exposure to different predictions adds to their enjoyment of the story-starter;

✳ how they might use chart entries to plan their own short mystery stories.

Our Predictions		
The Chicken-Coop Monster Might Be . . .	Because . . .	The Narrator Might Solve the Mystery By:
a wild animal	It smells; it may have "mean eyes."	Putting out some bait to lure the animal from the shed
a creaking door	She can hear it "swishing."	Listening carefully for the sound when the wind is blowing and when it is still

3. **Find Common Literary Elements** Well-wrought mystery stories share literary elements with other good fiction: vivid characterization; descriptions of the setting; events that grab the reader's interest. Discuss how the excerpt from "The Chicken-Coop Monster" fulfills these criteria.

SYNTHESIZING AND APPLYING

1. *Experiment with Transforming the Story-Starter* This activity provides a way for students to solidify their concept of what makes an effective mystery by contrasting the form with other genres and subgenres.

Invite students to work in groups of five or six. Copy the following chart on the chalkboard, or expand it into a reproducible to distribute. Ask groups to discuss and note ways to add to each "starter" in the style of the genre on the left. Responses will vary widely. Be sure to accept them all and to encourage students to be as creative and as imaginative as possible. Sample responses appear in parentheses.

Beginnings for Different Kinds of Writing	
Genre	**A Possible Beginning**
1. Report of Information	**In order to build a chicken coop you'll need** (wood, chicken-wire, straw, and chickens).
2. Fairy Tale	**Once upon a time, there was a princess who was trapped in a chicken coop. She** (had been put there by an unhappy hen who did not like the princess's habit of eating eggs for breakfast).
3. Poem	**The chicken said, "I hate this coop! "I want to sit on your front stoop." But when she opened the coop door,** (the chicken slipped on the kitchen floor. And, falling next into the sink, she said, "The coop is best, I think").
4. Mystery	**Farmer Brown was convinced that there were nothing but chickens in his coop. Imagine his surprise when Detective Fowl discovered** (a radio and a peanut butter sandwich in a chicken nest).

After groups have discussed their ideas with the class, suggest that students work independently or with a partner to implement one of the chart ideas by actually writing a fleshed-out story-starter. Students can read their introductions aloud, then ask the audience to guess which genre or subgenre they represent.

2. Listen/Read/View, Critique This activity requires just a short time to complete, and can be carried out at home as well as at school. If you choose the former, encourage students to get a family member involved in the activity. If you choose the latter, suggest that students work with a partner.

✻ Distribute copies of the *Mystery Web* on page 80 and review it with students. Then explain the assignment:

(a) While enjoying a mystery story, critique it carefully, using the web as a guide. Take notes.

(b) The mystery can be one that you listen to via radio or oral reading, one that you see on TV or on film, or one that you read independently.

(c) Be ready to tell your classmates

✻ the title of the mystery;

✻ the medium in which it was presented (i.e., book, TV show, radio drama);

✻ the basic situation in the mystery;

✻ how the mystery does, or does not, fulfill each of the criteria on the web.

3. Write an Original Mystery Story Through reading, responding to, and critiquing mysteries, and by noting how mysteries compare and contrast with other kinds of literature, most of your students will have gained enough background to write a mystery story that pleases them. Some students may prefer to write with partners or a small group of classmates, while other students may elect to write alone. Here are some strategies for getting started:

✻ Model your story on one you're familiar with. For example, take the beginning of "The Chicken-Coop Monster" as your model. Think of another realistic setting, another family situation, another scary challenge you've had to face. Review how the author of "The Chicken-Coop Monster" makes her story seem real and familiar. Try to do the same with your own mysteries.

✻ Base the situation and the solution on some tried-and-true mystery gimmicks: a secret visual or written code; a bizarre clue (a handkerchief with one part of a mono-gram ripped out; a watch that has stopped at a significant time; an idiosyncrasy of the perpetrator, such as a vast knowledge of literature; or a mastery of theatrical dis-guise), or the apparent innocence and helpfulness of a character who, in the long run, turns out to be the villain.

After drafting and revising, some students may wish to present their mysteries as short plays, or as taped "radio dramas." During follow-up class discussion, ask the audience to give their opinions about the strong points of the mystery. Ask the student writers to tell what they found most difficult in writing their mysteries.

4. *Delve Into Real-Life Mysteries* Present some mysteries that touch on different areas of your curriculum, and invite students to find out what factual research has uncovered about them. *Examples:*

✳ Is there <u>really</u> a Bigfoot? Loch Ness monster? Yeti?

✳ Is there really such a thing as the Bermuda Triangle?

✳ Whatever happened to Amelia Earhart?

✳ There are several documented cases of domestic pets, like cats and dogs, being able to track and find their owners over vast distances. How do you suppose the animals do that?

Students' research into these and other real-life mysteries will point out that truth is often stranger than fiction!

Suggest that students compile their reports on real-life mysteries into an anthology. Ask students to include a simple bibliography for each report, along with copies of pictures, graphs, maps, and other visual aides that can help readers understand the complexity of the mystery, the clues, and the varying answers.

CHAPTER 9

Modern Fantasy and Science Fiction

TEACHER OVERVIEW

It is best to study modern fantasy and science fiction together in order to develop concepts by contrast. This strategy can help the many students—even those skillful readers who quickly grasp the characteristics of other genres and subgenres—who have difficulty distinguishing between modern fantasy and science fiction.

The two kinds of stories are really quite different, as the web on page 91 indicates. If students confuse the types, it is usually due to

✳ Mislabeling: Many legitimate science-fiction stories have been plugged or publicized as "fantasy," and vice versa.

* The use of "imitation science" or futuristic-sounding elements in a fantasy tale (the "little-green-men-from-Mars" syndrome).

In primary grades, recognizing the difference between the two kinds of stories may not matter: after all, for younger children, a good read is a good read. Older students, however, have special concerns and abilities:

* They are becoming more aware of true science and its methodologies and discoveries; they often cite science fiction as their favorite kind of story to read and they want to write science fiction.

* They are also fond of reading fantasy, and like to inject fantasy elements into modern-day situations.

* They like to be "right." It matters to them that they can critique a story in an adult way, and write a story that fulfills the basic criteria of the genre and subgenre.

Science Fiction	*Modern Fantasy*
The major events might really happen, based on scientific facts that we know to be true.	The major events could not happen, according to science as we know it today.

PLOT

Time: Usually in the near or distant future **Place:** Earth, or another location that real scientists theorize may exist	**Time:** Usually right now **Place:** Usually a realistic place on Earth

SETTING

The characters solve a problem by using actual scientific data.	The characters solve a problem by using magic or impossible strategies.

PROBLEM

Fictional: but they act in ways that make sense from a scientific point of view	**Fictional:** but they act in ways that make sense in a fantasy situation

CHARACTERS

PRE-READING ACTIVITIES

1. Viewing Two Films Built Around a Common Theme, Exploration, and Discovery

Over a week's time, schedule time slots for your students to view two exemplary movies: Stanley Kubrick's science fiction classic, *2001: a Space Odyssey* and John Sayles' modern fantasy, *The Secret of Roan Inish*. Both are available in video stores. You may want to preview the films to determine which sections you wish your students to concentrate on.

You're probably familiar with the Kubrick film: astronauts of the very-near future, looking for evidence of other intelligent life in the universe, meet an unexpected impediment, a computer that won't follow their orders. While the astronauts accomplish their goal, they are forced to do so in a way they could not foresee.

In the more recent (1993) Sayles film, the ten-year-old heroine, who lives in modern-day Ireland, has a fantasy goal: to recover a little brother who was lost at sea some years ago. She encounters an unexpected, fantasy impediment: the seal-people, or silkies, who have adopted the boy as one of their own. In spite of this, the girl achieves her goal, though in a way that most viewers will agree is fantasy.

Preface viewing by distributing copies of the web and explaining that the class will view film versions of a science-fiction story and a fantasy story. Write the film titles on the chalkboard. Review the *Science Fiction/Fantasy Web* with the class and ask them to phrase questions for each element. Suggest that students make a chart like the one on page 93 to use as a viewing guide. After viewing one of the films, students can work with a partner to answer the questions on the chart before going on to the next film. Possible partner responses for some entries are given in parentheses.

Elements to Look for	Science Fiction *2001: A Space Odyssey*	Fantasy: *The Secret of Roan Inish*
Plot: Based on the science we know today, could the major events really happen?	(*Yes.* Space travel and computers are real. Some scientists are looking for clues to extraterrestrial life.)	(*No.* A baby lost at sea could not come back to life. Seals cannot turn into people.)
Setting: When and where is the story set?		
Problem: What problem do the characters deal with? How is the problem solved?	(Looking for extraterrestrial life: combating a rebellious computer)	(Bringing a lost child back to his family; convincing seal-people to let the child go)
Characters: Do the characters behave in ways that make sense in the story setting?		

Invite partners to share their completed charts with a larger group or with the whole class. Use any differences of opinion to spur lively debates, but insist that students support their ideas with details from the films or from their own knowledge and experience.

2. Drawing on the Literature: Critiquing Real Sci-Fi

Consult a local librarian and the *Annotated Bibliography*, page 111, to find three or four books that exemplify science fiction according to the criteria on the web. Ask students to work in small groups to read one of the books and prepare an oral or visual report that explains how the book adheres to the sci-fi criteria. *Example:*

Book: *River Rats*, by Carolyn Stevermer

• ***Information That We Know to Be True:*** Many nations possess nuclear weapons. If nuclear weapons were used, whole cities could be destroyed. In calamities like that, people would try to escape from the tragedy.

• ***Believable Characters:*** A boy—Tomcat—and his friends; they are all scared, anxious, and determined.

• **Believable Setting:** Time, the future—after the "flash," or nuclear explosion. Place, a paddle-wheel steamer on the Mississippi River.

• **A Realistic Problem to Solve:** How to find a safe place and reestablish a civilized life.

Ask groups to appoint a spokesperson to present a very brief summary of the story and the group's decisions about why the book qualifies as science fiction. Ask the audience to listen so as to tell (a) whether they agree with the group's reasoning; and (b) why they would or wouldn't want to read the book.

READING AND RESPONDING

Distribute copies of the excerpt from Ursula Le Guin's *A Ride on the Red Mare's Back* and the **Response Guide**. If possible, have the entire book available for your students to refer to and enjoy later on.

Summarize what has come before: the heroine's little brother has been kidnapped. The girl sets out to rescue him. She takes along her most beloved toy, a small wooden horse. Midway in her quest, the toy horse changes in a most remarkable way: she becomes a real, full-size mare!

Ask students to form reading/response groups of four or five. Have groups preview the **Response Guide** then read the excerpt together.

A Ride on the Red Mare's Back

by Ursula Le Guin

"There's a light," she whispered. The red mare bowed her neck and pushed on, climbing, one step at a time, though the snow was almost to her shoulders now.

She took one more step, and the snow was gone. She stood in a circle of light on a bare pavement before a stone door that stood open in the high side of a mountain. The snowy plain was behind them, and rocks and snow and cliffs in front of them, and the dark sky overhead.

"This is the High House," the red mare said, "where the trolls live."

The girl slipped from her back and stood beside her.

"Is my brother inside the mountain?" she asked.

The red mare nodded.

"Are there many trolls there?" she asked.

The red mare nodded.

"Are they afraid of you?" she asked.

The red mare shook her head. "But I am not afraid of them!" she said, stamping her hoof and shaking her leafy bridle. "So this is what we'll do, my girl. I'll call out the trolls, and tease them, and make them angry. They'll try to catch me. And while they're chasing me, you'll slip inside the mountain and find your brother and bring him out. But you must bring him out before the sun rises, for the trolls will all go back underground at the first light of dawn, lest they be caught in the sunlight and turned to stone. And I have only this one night with you."

"But if they catch you—" cried the girl.

"They'll be sorry," said the red mare. "Now, when they come out, take your chance and slip in like a mouse."

A Ride on the Red Mare's Back

RESPONSE GUIDE

Responders' names: _____ _____

_____ _____ _____

1. A little boy is kidnapped by trolls. What is real here? What is fantasy? Example: The kidnapped part could be real. But the troll part is fantasy because there are no such things as trolls. _____

_____

_____

_____

2. The heroine sets out to rescue her brother, and takes her favorite toy along. Does this seem realistic or unrealistic? Why? _____

_____

_____

_____

3. The toy horse changes into a real horse! What does the author do that makes the horse seem not only real, but very magical? _____

_____

_____

_____

4. How do you think the story will end? _____

_____

_____

_____

5. Sometimes people in fantasy stories discover a special strength that is their very own. What strength do you see in the heroine of this story? _____

_____

_____

_____

Responding Options

1. ***Encourage Students to Share Their Responses*** With luck, responses will vary widely, providing you and your students with an opportunity to see how book talks enrich and expand one's understanding of a text. Sample responses to questions 2–5 might read as follows: (2.) It seems realistic that the heroine might try to rescue her brother. As for taking a favorite toy along, maybe, if the toy was some kind of good-luck object, but it might also be "silly." (How could a toy help you to find someone?) (3.) The transformed toy horse not only moves like a real horse, but also talks like a human being. (4.) Most students will predict that the girl manages to rescue her brother. *Ask:* Who will help her pull this off? How is the ending you predict like a fairy-tale ending? What do you think will happen to the horse at the end of the story? (5.) Students may decide that the heroine's strength is courage, or love, or a sense of adventure, or a feeling of responsibility.

2. ***Find Common Literary Elements*** If your students have viewed and discussed the film *The Secret of Roan Inish*, you might ask them to discuss how the stories are alike. Mainly: (a) a sister searches for a lost brother; (b) fantastic obstacles—silkies/trolls—stand in their way, and (c) through fantastic strategies, the sisters achieve their goals: in one case with the help of a magic horse, and in the other by an appeal to the magical seals.

3. ***Contrast the "Villains" in Fantasy and Sci-Fi*** If your students have seen *2001: A Space Odyssey*, you might discuss with them how the villain (the malevolent computer HAL) compares with the villains (the trolls) in Le Guin's story. You might ask which villain is more believable? Which one is scarier? Why? How does your knowledge of science affect your answer?

SYNTHESIZING AND APPLYING

1. ***Using Science Knowledge to Plan a Science-Fiction Story*** This activity is designed to help student-writers use their backgrounds in science to help them construct an authentic science-fiction story. Pre-writing steps:

* Discuss the fantastic, "non-scientific" transformation in *A Ride on the Red Mare's Back* (a toy becomes real). Then move on to real-life transformations, e.g., polliwog to frog; larva to pupa to butterfly. Discuss how we know these latter transformations to be true as a result of long-time observations and conclusions of scientists.

* Ask students to form research/writing groups to discuss other "hot topics" in science today, such as

- growth hormones that increase size and weight;

- genetic alterations that can make living things more resistant to certain diseases;

- how different sections of a brain may be in charge of different functions, (e.g., a section for remembering, a section for visual input, etc.);

- how certain animals, like starfish and octopi, are able to regenerate an arm that has been destroyed.

✳ Ask research/writing groups to draft or outline a science-fiction story that centers around one of the science topics they've discussed. The draft should clearly state the science background and use it to develop the central problem in the story.

✳ Remind groups that a science-fiction story has the components of other fiction, i.e., a central problem, an interesting plot, a solution that makes sense within the context of the plot and main characters that the reader can relate to. You might suggest that groups do the preliminary planning of their story via a chart or story web. *Example:*

WICKED WINGS

Characters:
Dr. Anne Grimm;
her assistant, Ralph Roister;
detective Henry Hope;
Nancy Antt, a newspaper reporter

Setting:
The Archway Butterfly Museum;
twenty years from now.

CENTRAL PROBLEM:
Is it a good idea to tamper with nature?

SCIENCE BACKGROUND:
Scientists are investigating substances
that can increase growth
and intelligence.

Plot: Dr. Grimm uses hormones to create a butterfly with a tweny-foot wing span. The butterfly gets loose and looks for a flower. It lands on a woman's flowered hat, and the woman almost suffocates.

Resolution of Problem:
Dr. Grimm captures the butterfly. She injects it with a drug that will heighten its intelligence so that it can discriminate between real flowers and fake ones. BUT . . . Who knows what a smart butterfly will decide to do?

Suggest that research/writing groups confer with other classmates to determine whether their outlines and drafts adhere to the requirements of science fiction. After students have conferred, revised, and edited, ask them to appoint classmates to design and construct an anthology of their original science fiction.

2. Using Real Life to Plan a Modern Fantasy Story Introduce this activity by asking students to recall and give examples of the main ingredients of a fairy tale. Points you might discuss:

✳ The heroine or hero—rich or poor—is usually someone with quite ordinary characteristics. For example, Cinderella is just a young girl who needs some love.

✳ The heroine or hero has a goal that we can sympathize with. For example, a prince wishes to be accepted for who he is ("The Frog Prince"), Dumpkin (in "The Three Feathers") wants to be respected by his father and his brothers.

✳ Something "magical" happens that enables the heroine or hero to attain the goal. For example, a fairy godparent appears, the answers to three riddles are revealed, or some brave action proves the hero or heroine worthy of the reward.

To help students realize that all these ingredients can be part of a modern fantasy set in today's world, discuss how the ingredients appear in *A Ride on the Red Mare's Back*.

✳ The heroine is an ordinary girl.

✳ The heroine has a goal we can sympathize with: to rescue her little brother.

✳ Something magical happens to help her attain her goal: a toy horse becomes real and fends off those who stand in her way.

3. Suggest That Students Present Their Final Story in Dramatic Form To this end, students can work in groups of five or six to develop ideas, draft and complete a script, and perform their play. As a pre-writing strategy, you might supply an idea source bank and ask the class to brainstorm examples of each idea.

Idea Sources for Modern Fantasies

• Updates of traditional fairy tales. *Example:* The little mermaid is now a modern-day scuba diver.

• Sequels to modern fantasies you've read or viewed. *Example:* The heroine in *The Secret of Roan Inish* wishes she could become a seal for a while.

• Fantasy versions of real-life news stories. *Example:* Air Force I, with the President aboard, sets off for Europe, but lands instead in a mysterious, undiscovered land.

- A fantasy version of realistic fiction you've enjoyed. *Example:* The hero in Beverly Cleary's *Dear Mr. Henshaw* visits magical places and has impossible adventures.

• A fantasy journal, transforming actual events from journal entries.

4. *Viewing Critically to Detect Fantasy* Have students and their families keep a written record of fantasy on television. To simplify and organize note taking, students can use the following chart.

Fantasy in TV Programs and Commercials		
Day of the week	Name of TV program or commercial	What was fantastic?
Monday		
Tuesday		
Wednesday		
Thursday		
Friday		

Small groups of students can share and compare their completed charts, using these questions to guide discussion:

1. Which TV stories and commercials were <u>meant</u> to be fantasy?
2. Which were meant to be realistic, but had some elements of fantasy that made them unbelievable? Could these stories or commercials be confusing? Explain.
3. Suppose you were a TV script-writer. Which of the stories or commercials on your chart would you re-write? Why?

Annotated Bibliography:

Some Selected Titles

I've selected exemplary titles that (1) provide good background and follow-up for the concepts about genres presented in this book, (2) appeal to middle-grade students with a variety of interests and reading skills, and (3) are likely to be available through school or local libraries. There are, of course, hundreds of other great books in each category. You can urge your students to make their own annotated bibliographies, listing their favorite already-read books, and adding new titles as they read, discuss, and critique them.

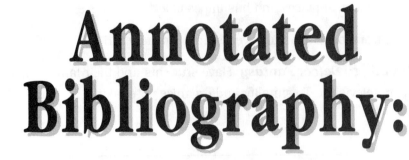

POETRY

A (*) indicates a single-author collection; most of these are built around themes implied in the titles, and are good departure points for students' anthologies of poems built around curricular topics. The other books listed are general anthologies, some of them also thematic; use them for reference and read-aloud sessions.

* **Fleischmann, Paul.** *Joyful Noise: Poems for Two Voices.* Harper, 1988.

* **Greenfield, Eloise.** *Night on Neighborhood Street.* Dial, 1991.

Harrison, Michael and Christopher Stuart-Clark, comps. *The Oxford Book of Animal Poems.* Oxford, 1992.

Hopkins, Lee Bennett, comp. *Through Our Eyes: Poems and Pictures About Growing Up.* Little, Brown, 1992. And *Hand in Hand: An American History Through Poetry.* Simon and Schuster, 1995.

Koch, Kenneth and Kate Farrell, comps. *Talking to the Sun.* Holt, 1985

Larrick, Nancy, comp. *Piping Down the Valleys Wild.* Delacorte, 1985.

Nye, Naomi Shihab, comp. *The Same Sky: A Collection of Poems from Around the World.* Four Winds, 1992.

Philip, Neil. *Singing America: Poems That Define a Nation.* Viking, 1995.

* **Prelutsky, Jack.** *The New Kid on the Block.* Greenwillow, 1984.

Schwartz, Alvin, comp. *And the Green Grass Grew All Around.* Harper, 1992.

* **Silverstein, Shel.** *Where the Sidewalk Ends.* Harper, 1974.

* **Yolen, Jane.** *Bird Watch.* Philomel, 1991.

BIOGRAPHY

Cummings, Pat. *Talking with Artists.* Bradbury, 1993. Through interviews, Cummings presents the lives and thoughts of fourteen famous illustrators of children's books. Because the artists responded to identical questions, readers can easily compare and contrast backgrounds and approaches to art. The book also serves as a fine model for students who wish to interview as a prelude to writing a biography.

Freedman, Russell. *Indian Chiefs.* Holiday, 1992. The biographies of six western chiefs—Red Cloud, Satanta, Quannah Parker, Washakie, Chief Joseph, and Sitting Bull—all revolve around an essential question: To save one's people, is it wiser to capitulate to whites, or to resist them in an attempt to preserve hunting grounds and a unique way of life?

Freedman, Russell. *Kids at Work: Lewis Hine and the Crusade Against Child Labor.* Clarion, 1994. A biography of Lewis Hine, an American photographer who worked in the first half of the twentieth century. Hine's main concern was for the children who were forced to labor long hours in factories and mines. He dedicated himself to opening the public's eye to the plight of these children.

Fritz, Jean. *You Want Women to Vote, Lizzie Stanton?* Putnam,1995. Early in life, Elizabeth Cady Stanton saw that "girls didn't count for much." She spent her long life changing this situation. Young readers will empathize with Stanton's struggles to overcome not only societal prejudices, but also her own shyness.

Livingston, Myra Cohn. *Let Freedom Ring.* Holiday, 1993. Livingston uses the ballad form to tell the story of *Dr. Martin Luther King, Jr.* She uses many quotes from his sermons and speeches.

Murphy, Jim. *The Boys' War: Confederate and Union Soldiers Talk About the Civil War.* Clarion, 1990. Murphy has gathered the oral histories of underage soldiers (boys 16 years old and younger) to show the Civil War through their eyes. The photo-essay approach makes the boys' experiences vivid, and may also inspire your students to research and use visuals in their own reports of information.

Ransom, Candice F. *Listening to Crickets: A Story About Rachel Carson.* Carolrhoda, 1993. The biography shows how Carson's love and concern for her friends was reflected in her love and concern for the environment.

Your more mature students may want to make such a real-life/work connection in biographies they critique, and in biographical anecdotes they write.

Stanley, Fay. *The Last Princess: The Story of Princess Ka'iulani of Hawaii.* Four Winds, 1992. Provides a good overview of Hawaiian history and the life of a courageous princess. Acts also as a springboard for student discussions of women's issues, monarchy, prejudice, and colonization.

AUTOBIOGRAPHY

Bulla, Clyde Robert. *A Grain of Wheat: A Writer Begins.* Godine, 1985. Bulla has written a number of books popular with young readers. His fans will enjoy finding out how he discovered his vocation.

Cleary, Beverly. *A Girl From Yamhill.* Morrow, 1988. Cleary relates her life story in the anecdotal, whimsical way she uses in her fiction for young people. Her details about the wonder of "ordinary" people and events may inspire students to write about their own lives.

Frank, Anne. *The Diary of Anne Frank.* This, of course, is the *sine qua non* of a journal that records not only the universal feelings of a preteen, but also the tragic times in which the young writer was caught up. Students might discuss how "private" journals may eventually add vital information to our understanding of historic events.

Peter Roop and Connie Roop eds. *I, Columbus.* Walker, 1991. The Roops have selected and edited Robert Fuson's translation of Columbus's own log to make an exciting journal that—along with the end-paper maps—makes history come alive for young readers. Your students can discuss how journals make history real and form groups to find other sources of historical information.

Lawlor, Veronica. *I Was Dreaming to Come to America: Memories from the Ellis Island Oral History Project.* Viking, 1995. Fifteen first-person narratives of people who arrived at Ellis Island as children between 1897 and 1925.

Lyons, Mary E. *Letters from a Slave Girl: The Story of Harriet Jacobs.* Scribner's, 1992. Jacobs wrote her autobiography in 1861, vividly describing her efforts to go North to freedom. Lyons has selected entries and passages that highlight Jacobs's struggle. Your students might discuss how a journal writer—keeping notes for her or his own interest—may eventually contribute to an understanding of history.

Peet, Bill. *Bill Peet: An Autobiography.* Houghton, 1990. Most kids love Peet's illustrations, and the budding artists in your room will enjoy his recountings of what happened when he drew cartoons in the margins of his textbooks, and of his career as an artist in the Disney studios. Some students might use Peet's storyboard techniques to make storyboards of big events in Peet's own life, or in their own lives.

Thaxter, Celia. *Celia's Island Journal,* edited and illustrated by Loretta Krupinski. Little, Brown, 1992. Thaxter was seven years old when, in 1839, her family moved into a lighthouse for several years. What's to report in such an isolated existence? Your students who claim they have nothing to write about may get some ideas from observant Celia.

REPORTS OF INFORMATION

Ancona, George. *Powwow.* Harcourt, Brace Jovanovich, 1993. Ancona, a photographer and a writer, collected facts about powwows—gatherings of Native American groups who perform traditional music and dance—by attending the Crow Fair in Montana. This work is a collection of his photos and his writings on powwows.

Cone, Molly. *Come Back, Salmon.* Sierra Club, 1993. A vivid account of how students and teachers at Jackson Elementary School in Everett, Washington, used clout and hard work to change a dying river back into a salmon spawning ground. The step-by-step narration is a good model for informational reports on various subjects. The we-can-do-it theme may inspire your students to get active in local environmental situations that concern them.

Freedman, Russell. *Buffalo Hunt.* Holiday House, 1989. Freedman points out the historical role of buffalo in Native American life, legend, and economy. Included are great paintings of buffalo and the hunt. The combination of text and visuals may inspire your students to use similar combinations in their own informational reports.

George, Jean Craighead. *The Moon of the Bears.* Harper, 1993. The report traces a black bear's year through the month of February, when she gives birth to twin cubs. Like other books in George's *Thirteen Moons* series, this one is characterized by glowing, accurate descriptions and a clear narrative line. These are qualities your students may want to emulate in their own reports of information.

Murphy, Jim. *The Great Fire.* Scholastic, 1995. The story of the Chicago fire of 1871 comes together vividly through the author's straight narrative, first-hand accounts of survivors, newspaper stories, and contemporaneous lithographs and photos.

Peters, Russell M. *Clambake.* Photos by John Madama. Lerner, 1993. Appanaug, or clambake, is a traditional ceremony of Wampanoag Indians of the New England coast. Like *Powwow* the report is made from the point of view of a child and an older relative. You might encourage students to use this approach in an informational report about a ceremony or celebration of their own culture.

Quinlan, Susan E. *The Case of the Mummified Pigs: And Other Mysteries in Nature.* Boyds, 1995. The text tells of fourteen mysterious situations in nature and shows how scientists work, from theory to proof—to account for them. The cases are truly fascinating, as are the explanations of how scientists network, gather clues and data, and work toward solutions.

Siegal, Beatrice. *George and Martha Washington at Home in New York.* Four Winds, 1990. For sixteen months, New York was the new nation's capital. Siegal emphasizes the social ambiance there, as well as political events. This makes the Washingtons' life seem very real. Your students might reenact the first presidential inauguration; draw maps of NYC as it existed in the Washingtons' time there; research and report on Philadelphia as it appeared during the next ten years as the nation's capital or find out why and how a permanent capital was designed along the Potomac River.

Swan, Robert. *Destination: Antarctica.* Scholastic, 1988. In 1986, Swan and his companions trekked 900 miles from Antarctica to the South Pole, to duplicate Robert Scott's 1912 journey. The brilliant photos that clarify the text will suggest to your students how to use visuals to enhance their own informational reports.

REALISTIC FICTION IN A MODERN SETTING

Baille, Allan. *Little Brother*. Viking, 1985. In Cambodia, two brothers are separated as they make their way to the Thai border to escape the Khmer Rouge.

Banks, Jacqueline Turner. *Egg-Drop Blues*. Houghton, 1995. Jury Jenkins helps his twin brother, Judge, who suffers from dyslexia, win an award at a science fair. The school and home situations are wonderfully realistic, and the brothers are great friends.

Danziger, Paula. *Earth to Matthew*. Delacorte, 1991. Preteen Matthew struggles with growing up in suburban America. The humor is light-hearted, and the dialogue on target.

Ellis, Sarah. *Out of the Blue*. McElderry, 1995. Megan discovers that she has a much-older sister whom her mother gave up at birth and who has now sought out her biological family. This is an empathetic, graceful, humorous treatment of a modern situation.

Fenner, Carol. *Yolanda's Genius*. McElderry, 1995. Yolanda is convinced that her six-year-old brother is a musical genius, and sets out to prove it. She's rewarded when he performs at the annual Chicago blues festival.

Hamilton, Virginia. *Drylongso*. Harcourt, 1992. The problems that drought causes for farmers are cleverly presented in the story of a homeless boy who helps his benefactors restore their land.

Pinkney, Andrea Davis. *Hold Fast to Dreams*. Morrow, 1995. When her father gets a great new job, Dee Willis has to leave her beloved Baltimore home and move to Connecticut where "everybody's white." This first-person narrative tells a convincing story about a twelve-year-old's adjustments to her family's pursuit of the American dream.

Pinkwater, Jill. *Tails of the Bronx: A Tale of the Bronx*. Macmillan, 1991. Funny in spots, heartbreaking in others, this is the story of some kids who want to rescue homeless cats, and instead encounter the problems of homeless people.

Soto, Gary. *Boys at Work*. Delacorte, 1995. In this sequel to *The Pool Party*, two ten-year-old boys try to raise money during their summer vacation. The book has an interesting twist, and Soto's usual facility for integrating Latino culture with the universal feelings of preteens.

Yep, Laurence. *Thief of Hearts*. Harper 1995. Stacy, a Chinese-American girl, is asked to take care of initiating Hong Chu'un, a new classmate from China, to school life. The girls encounter realistic problems that have to do with the question of loyalty to one's heritage. The first-person narrative is both moving and funny.

HISTORICAL FICTION

Cech, John. *My Grandmother's Journey.* Bradbury, 1991. The heroine's adventure begins in pre-revolutionary Russia, continues through the Russian Revolution, includes capture by the Nazis, and concludes happily in America.

Dorris, Michael. *Morning Girl.* Hyperion, 1992. The setting is a Bahamian isle just before Columbus's 1492 landing, and the main characters are a young girl and her brother going about their day-to-day tasks. In the final pages, "Morning Girl" greets the foreign sailors who suddenly arrive on shore. Questions such as "What do you think will happen next" will provide students with much to think about and discuss.

Gray, Elizabeth Janet. *Adam of the Road.* Puffin 1987. Adam's search for his father and for Nick, his stolen dog, leads him into encounters with pilgrims, rich merchants, farmers, thieves, and other people who travel the roads of medieval Europe.

Krensky, Stephen. *The Printer's Apprentice.* Delacorte, 1995. Gus, apprenticed in 1734 to a conservative New York printer, has to think hard about Peter Zenger, an outspoken competitor who criticizes British rule in the American colonies. The issue of freedom of speech is presented clearly, and in a way that captures the flavor of the times.

Lowry, Lois. *Number the Stars.* Houghton, 1989. A ten-year-old girl becomes part of the Danish Resistance during World War II and helps a friend escape the Holocaust.

Temple, Frances. *The Ramsey Scallop.* Orchard, 1994. The setting is medieval Europe. A young girl and her betrothed, both wary about a future marriage arranged by their fathers, join a pilgrimage from England to Santiago de Compostelo. They become friends as they share adventures and their reactions to them.

Uchida, Yoshiko. *Journey Home.* Atheneum, 1978. Yuki and her Japanese-American family attempt to get settled again in California after their internment in a Utah concentration camp during World War II.

FOLK LITERATURE

Collections:

Belting, Natalie. *The Earth Is on a Fish's Back.* Holt, 1965. Twenty-one origin legends and myths from around the world.

DeSpain, Pleasant. *Thirty-Three Multicultural Tales To Tell.* August, 1993.

Hamilton, Virginia. *In the Beginning: Creation Stories from Around the World.* Harcourt, 1988.

Mayo, Margaret. *Magical Tales from Many Lands.* Dutton, 1993.

Yolen, Jane. *Favorite Folktales from Around the World.* Pantheon, 1986.

Focus On Specific Cultures:

In the Americas

Belting, Natalie M. *Moon Was Tired of Walking.* Houghton, 1992. Origin myths from ten South American tribes.

Bruhac, Joseph. *Flying with the Eagle, Racing the Great Bear: Stories from Native North America.* Bridgewater, 1993.

de Paola, Tomie. *The Legend of the Bluebonnet.* Putnam, 1983. And *The Legend of the Indian Paintbrush.* Putnam, 1987.

Hamilton, Virginia. *The People Could Fly.* Knopf, 1985. African-American legends and folktales.

Haviland, Virginia. *North American Legends.* Putnam, 1979. Legends of African-Americans, European-Americans, and Native-Americans.

Martinez, Alejandro Cruz. *The Woman Who Outshone the Sun.* Children's Book Press, 1991. A Zapotec legend in English and Spanish.

Taylor, C.J. *How We Saw the World: Nine Native Stories of the Way Things Began.* Tundra, 1993.

In Asia and India

Birdseye, Tom. *A Song of Stars.* Holiday, 1990. Chinese myth of the stars Vega and Altair.

Chatterjee, Debjani. *The Elephant-Headed God and Other Hindu Tales.* Oxford, 1992.

Fang, Linda. *The Ch'i-lin Purse: A collection of Ancient Chinese Stories.* Farrar, 1995.

Ginsburg, Mirra. *The Chinese Mirror.* Harcourt, 1988. A Korean tale.

Hong, Lily T. *How the Ox Star Fell from Heaven.* Whitman, 1990. A tale from China.

Lee, Jeanne. *The Toad Is the Uncle of Heaven.* Holt, 1985. A story from Vietnam.

Louie, Ai-Ling. *Yeh-Shen: A Cinderella Story from China.* Philomel, 1982.

Uchida, Yoshiko. *The Sea of Gold and Other Tales from Japan.* Gregg, 1988.

Vuong, Lynette Dyer. *Sky Legends of Vietnam.* Harper, 1993.

In Africa and Egypt

Aardema, Verna. *Rabbit Makes a Monkey Out of Lion.* Dial, 1989.

Appiah, Peggy. *Tales of an Ashanti Father.* Beacon, 1989. Trickster stories from Ghana.

Ashford, Jules. *The Myth of Isis and Osiris.* Barefoot, 1993.

Clayton, Bess. *The Truth About the Moon.* Houghton, 1983. Several African moon legends.

Climo, Shirley. *The Egyptian Cinderella.* Crowell, 1989.

Dayrell, Elphinstone. *Why the Sun and Moon Live in the Sky.* Houghton, 1990. A Nigerian legend.

Haley, Gail. *A Story, a Story.* Atheneum, 1970. Tales from several African cultures.

Kimmel, Eric. *Anansi and the Moss-Covered Rock.* Holiday House, 1990.

Williams, Sheron. *And in the Beginning.* Atheneum, 1992. A Swahili folktale.

In the Middle East

Al-Saleh, Khairat. *Fabled Cities, Princes & Jinn from Arab Myths and Legends.* Schlocken, 1985.

Lewis, Naomi. *Stories from the Arabian Nights.* Holt, 1987.

Mayer, Maranna. *Aladdin and the Enchanted Lamp.* Macmillan, 1985.

Zeman, Ludmilla. *The Revenge of Ishtar.* Tundra, 1993. The Gilgamesh myth from ancient Mesopotamia.

In Europe

de Gerez, Toni. *Louhi, Witch of North Farm: A Finnish Tale.* Viking, 1986. A retelling of part of the Kalevala, Finland's great epic.

de Paola, Tomi. *Prince of the Dolomites.* Harcourt, 1980. An Italian moon legend.

Evslin, Bernard. *The Minotaur.* Chelsea House, 1987. A retelling of the Greek legend.

Fonteyn, Margot. *Swan Lake.* Harcourt, 1989. The Russian legend on which the ballet is based.

Littedale, Freya. *Peter and the North Wind.* Scholastic, 1988. A tale from Norway.

McDermott, Beverly Brodsky. *The Golem: A Jewish Legend.* Lippincott, 1976. Tales from Czechoslovakia.

San Souci, Robert D. *Young Merlin.* Doubleday, 1990. An introduction to the Arthurian legends.

Shute, Linda. *Clever Tom and the Leprechaun.* Lothrop, 1988. A retelling of an Irish folktale.

Sutcliff, Rosemary. *Black Ships Before Troy: The Story of the Iliad.* Delacorte, 1993.

Yolen, Jane. *The Greyling.* Philomel, 1991. Selchi legends from Scotland about seals that take on human forms.

MYSTERY

Single Titles

Brenner, Barbara. *Mystery of the Disappearing Dogs.* Knopf, 1982. Twins set out to find their kidnapped dog.

Bulla, Clyde R. *The Ghost of Windy Hill.* Scholastic, 1990. A family sets out to prove a house isn't haunted, then encounter some eerie events.

Hamilton, Virginia. *The House of Dies Drear.* Macmillan, 1984. A classic suspense story in which a history professor and his son investigate the mystery of their rented house, which was formerly a station on the Underground Railroad.

Kastner, Erich. *Emil and the Detectives.* Scholastic, 1992. This classic mystery for young readers stars a boy and one hundred detectives pursuing a thief through the streets of Berlin.

McKissack, Patricia C. *The Dark Thirty.* Knopf, 1992. The dark thirty refers to the half-hour children have to get home before night falls. These ten tales (concluding with "The Chicken-Coop Monster") draw upon stories African-American children in the rural south told each other in that magical time between day and night.

Perske, Robert. *Don't Stop the Music.* Abingdon, 1986. Joe and Jessica (twins who have cerebral palsy) investigate an auto-theft ring.

Salway, Lance. *Beware, This House Is Haunted.* Scholastic, 1990. For the heroine, joke-notes turn out to lead to something realistically terrifying.

Slote, Alfred. *Finding Buck McHenry.* Harper, 1991. Eleven-year-old Jason is convinced that the school custodian, Mack Henry, is actually Buck McHenry, the famous pitcher from the old Negro League.

Vivelo, Jackie. *Chills Run Down My Spine.* Dorling Kindersley, 1994. Nine short mysteries and ghost stories that are bound to send shivers down your spine. Great for read-alouds.

Series

As you know, series can not only turn kids on to mysteries, but also on to the pleasures of reading itself, as they track through assorted adventures with favorite heroines and heroes. Some series to suggest:

Adler, David A. *The Fourth Floor Twins.* Viking.

Eastman, David. *Sherlock Homes Mysteries.* Troll. Conan-Doyle's stories adapted for young readers.

Keene, Carolyn. *Nancy Drew.* Scholastic.

Miller, Marvin. *You Be the Jury.* Scholastic. In each book, readers are given ten courtroom mysteries and are challenged to predict the judge's verdict.

Sharmat, Marjorie. *Nate the Great.* Dell. Young Nate wears a Sherlock Holmes outfit as he conducts his sleuthing.

Warner, Gertrude Chandler. *The Boxcar Children.* Scholastic. These four siblings have a taste and talent for solving mysteries.

MODERN FANTASY

Bradshaw, Gillian. *The Land of Gold.* Greenwillow, 1992. Princess Kandaki of ancient Nubia strives to recapture her throne from the evil Shabako. She's assisted by a dragon and other motley beings.

Le Guin, Ursula K. *A Ride on the Red Mare's Back.* Orchard, 1992. A sci-fi writer turns her attention to the fantasy that exists in this world.

Mahy, Margaret. *Underrunners.* Viking, 1992. Tristram meets a mysterious girl named Winola who lives in a twisting, subterranean world. A dazzling plot line!

McMurtry, Stan. *The Bunjee Adventure.* Scholastic, 1986. Two children go back to prehistoric days via a time machine to rescue their feckless father. **Also with time-travel themes:** Greer and Ruddick's *Max and Me and the Wild West.* Harcourt, 1988; Madeleine L'Engle's *A Wrinkle in Time.* Farrar, 1962.

Norman, Roger. *Albion's Dream.* Delacorte, 1992. Edward finds an ancient, homemade game (Albion's Dream), plays it with friends, and finds himself caught up in a fantasy battle between good and evil.

Wynne-Jones, Tim. *Some of the Kinder Planets.* Orchard/Kroupa, 1995. Nine short stories begin with ordinary situations kids will recognize, then move to quirky, alternate universes of the mind. Students will enjoy the wild logic and the unforgettable characters.

SCIENCE FICTION

Asch, Frank. *Journey to Terezor.* Holiday, 1989. First volume in the Orb Trilogy. Man and his parents escape a flood and go to live on Planet S-5's earth colony.

Christopher, John. *When the Tripods Came.* Dutton, 1988. Much food for thought for mature readers. Alien beings come to Earth and impose a new order.

Erlanger, Ellen. *Issac Asimov: Scientist and Storyteller.* Lerner, 1987. This biography can be most helpful to your students who want to explore how to blend solid science with effective storytelling strategies.

Lowry, Lois. *The Giver.* Dell, 1993. The hero wrestles with core questions: Is it possible to create a "perfect" world? What constraints to freedom might that involve?

Service, Pamela. *Winter of Magic's Return.* Macmillan, 1985. The story is set five-hundred years after a nuclear holocaust. There is an aura of Arthurian legend as humans try to set up a beneficent civilization.

Wisler, G. Clifton. *The Antrian Messenger.* Dutton, 1986. (And its sequel, *The Seer*, 1988). Poses intriguing questions about the possibility of other intelligent beings in the universe.